Weeve i...
part of so... ...l.

Sign up for an ac... ...e
future of l... ...g

WWW.WEEVE.IE

25%

**Upload books of
your choice**

**Dynamically adjust
translation difficulty**

**Real-time
pronunciations**

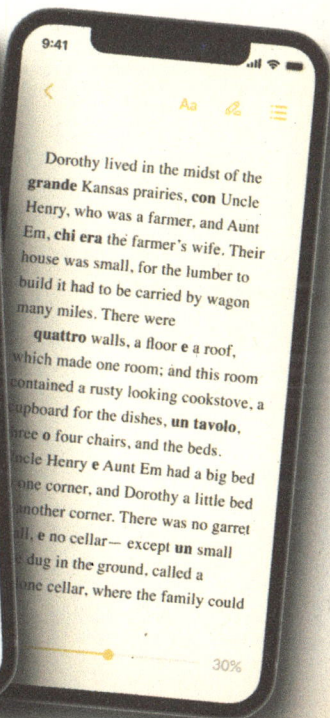

9:41

Reading Now

Learn
ITALIAN
**THE WONDERFUL
WIZARD of OZ**
The Wonderful Wizard of Oz

GERMAN
**SHERLOCK
HOLMES**
Sherlock Holmes: The H...

Learn
PORTUGUES
**THE WONDERFUL
WIZARD of O...**
The Wonderful Wizard of...

Weeve Library
New collection of upcycled and original Weeve titles

SPANISH
**SHERLOCK
HOLMES**
Sherlock Holmes: The H...

SPANISH
**THE WONDERFUL
WIZARD of OZ**
The Wonderful Wizard of Oz

SPANISH
**THE GREAT
GATSBY**
The Great Gatsby

See all

Library   Challenges   Weeve Store   Statistics

9:41

Aa

Dorothy lived in the midst of the **grande** Kansas prairies, **con** Uncle Henry, who was a farmer, and Aunt Em, **chi era** the farmer's wife. Their house was small, for the lumber to build it had to be carried by wagon many miles. There were **quattro** walls, a floor **e** a roof, which made one room; and this room contained a rusty looking cookstove, a cupboard for the dishes, **un tavolo**, three o four chairs, and the beds. Uncle Henry **e** Aunt Em had a big bed in one corner, and Dorothy a little bed in another corner. There was no garret at all, **e** no cellar— except **un** small hole dug in the ground, called a cyclone cellar, where the family could

30%

Welcome to Weeve

Here at Weeve, we believe that traditional language education, with its painful memorisation, repetition and tedious grammar classes, have failed students around the world in their pursuit of learning a new language. Over 50 years of education research supports us on this. Studies show that the best way of encouraging language acquisition is reading and listening to engaging and accessible content. With that vision in mind, we created Weeve. Our method allows you to learn up to 20 words per hour in your target language – we are confident you'll never want to learn languages in any other way. Thank you for supporting us on this journey.

How to Use Weeve

Weeved Words

The sentences in this novel have foreign words weaved into the English sentences. Introducing foreign words within the context of an English sentence allows our brain to form a contextual representation of that foreign word without needing to translate it. At the start of our books only a few words are translated, as you progress, getting lost in the world of fantasy, more and more translated words are added.

Read - Don't Translate

When you come across a foreign word weaved into a sentence resist the urge to translate the word back to English. Your brain will automatically do this at first, but with practice this skill can be mastered.

Context is Key

Read the foreign words as they are written and try to understand it in the context of the story. Translating disrupts the flow of the story, and it is these flow states where pleasure and language acquisition will occur. Don't worry about your speed of acquisition - trust the process.

Go with the Flow

Language acquisition is a subconscious process that happens when we read and listen to interesting things that we understand. All you have left to do is enjoy the story, try not to think too much about the words and you will acquire them faster.

Vocab Tables

You will find vocabulary tables at the end of chapters - consider these milestones, showing the weaved words you have read during that chapter. Quickly double check you understand them and continue learning! These vocab tables also offer the International Phonetic Alphabet (IPA) phonetic pronunciation of the word.

Weeve's Story

The idea for Weeve was born when Cian was having a bath and an apple hit him on the head. Four years ago, Cian spoke only English and decided to try and learn Portuguese. For two years he tried and failed to learn the language using the traditional methods available out there – flashcards, language learning apps, grammar lessons. Despite having over 5000 words memorised, Cian found his speech was still slow and his comprehension was poor.

Frustrated at his lack of progress, Cian began to research second language acquisition. The core message that research and academia has proven over the past 50 years is simple - *you only acquire language when you read and listen to content you understand.* The problem was that there is no option for beginners to get their hands on comprehensible input as they do not have the foundational knowledge required to jump into reading short stories and novels.

So, inspired by the evidence that bilingual students learn best in settings where languages are blended together, Cian began a six-month long journey of researching, trialling, and developing the first ever Weeve book (a Swedish version of *The Wheel of Time*). He pulled in Evan, who had had a terrible experience learning languages in school, and the two of them began developing the idea. As the first Weeve guinea pigs, the pair knew they were onto a winner when they were capable of learning their first 400 Swedish words with no effort, no memorisation and no pain.

The hunger for Weeve's products was evident from the launch of the first book, *Learn Spanish with Sherlock Holmes*, in July 2020. Since launch, Weeve have had an immensely exciting time. The collection has expanded to include eleven languages and has sold over 2500 copies. The Weeve team joined a Trinity student accelerator program, which connected them with Sinéad. Sinéad was a member of the judging panel at a start-up competition when she first came across the Weeve duo. It was love at first sight and just three days after the competition she was officially part of the gang.

The fourth member of our team, Oisin joined over the summer of 2021. A computer scientist determined to digitise the Weeve method so it can reach global scale. Currently working on an application that will allow for complete dynamic control over translations within your weeve.

The response to our Weeve books around the globe has been immense winning a number of awards like the LEO ICT Award and placing in Spark Crowdfundings top 100 most amibitious companies. With the founders appearing in the Sunday Independant's 30 Under 30.

Weeve wants to make languages ridiculously simple and accessible to everyone. We hope you enjoy it as much as we do, and stick around for our journey.

Meet the Team

Cian McNally

Cian is a Psychology graduate from Trinity College Dublin and a language learning enthusiast. In the past 4 years he has gone from speaking only English to being able to read many novels in Portuguese, Spanish and German, as well as short stories in Swedish and Italian. When he's not revolutionising the language learning industry, he is probably found playing chess or talking about how tall he is.

Evan McGloughlin

Evan is a Neuroscience graduate from Trinity College Dublin and has a passion for learning and education. He runs a youtube channel where he attempts to make practical neuroscience accessible and entertaining. He always despised how languages were taught in school always thinking it felt very unnatural. When Cian came to him with the idea for Weeve it instantly resonated with him as a more natural and effective approach.

Sinead McAleer

Sinéad lives a double life – working in a bank by day and growing Weeve by night. After graduating from Computer Science & Business at Trinity College Dublin, Sinéad moved to London where she now leads our international office (aka a desk in the corner of her bedroom). She has a passion for start-ups, technology and vegan/vegetarian experimentation!

Oisín T. Morrin

Oisín loves all things at the intersection of language and technology. This brought him to study Computer Science, Linguistics and Irish at TCD as an All-Ireland Scholar. Japanese, Irish and Python are his love languages, and he also dabbles in Korean, German and Scot's Gaelic. Outside of Weeve, Oisín can invariably be found with a new book in one hand and a coffee in the other.

How to Have a Perfect Accent

You may have never seen the IPA before but it's the universal way to perfectly write pronunciations. The aim of the IPA is to provide a unique symbol for each distinctive sound in a language. You already know most of these symbols as they are letters in English. If you familiarise yourself with the other ~15 of these symbols you'll always be able to pronounce foreign words perfectly without having to learn more than 140 spelling rules.

IPA Guide

b like b in about

β like b in about also but without your lips fully closing

ð like th in this

ɣ like g in again without your tongue touching the roof of your mouth

ʃ like sh in sheep

ʎ like ll in million

ʒ like s in pleasure

j like the y in you

x like the ch in Loch Ness

ɐ like u in purse

ɛ like e in set

i like ee in see

ɔ like o in off

ɱ like m in comfort

ŋ like ng in sing

ɲ like ny in canyon

tʃ like ch in chips

o like o in row

u like oo in boot

ɾ this is the flipped r which isn't in English. If you say the word "butter" in an American accent "budder" the sound of the "tt" is almost the same.

r is the thrilled r sound

weeve

Book Publishing Details

Exclusive book publishing rights pertain to copyright ©Weeve 2022

Design, production, editing, and illustration credits:
Logo and Cover Design by Aaron Connolly

Cover and Interior Illustrations by Otherworld Creations, Leoramos
www.fiverr.com/Otherworlder
www.fiverr.com/Leoramos

Editing, production:
Weeve
Translation:
Violetta Caballero (Weeve Editor)
Lauren Cusack (Weeve Editor)

Fonts:
Recoletta, Times New Roman, Tomarik

Publisher Address:
31 Millers Lane, Skerries, Co. Dublin, Ireland
Author Website:
https://weeve.ie/
Country in which the book was printed:
United States, United Kingdom

weeve

SHERLOCK HOLMES
A STUDY IN SCARLET

PART 1

THE REMINISCENCES OF
JOHN H. WATSON, M.D.,

LATE OF THE ARMY MEDICAL DEPARTMENT

1

MR. SHERLOCK HOLMES

En the year 1878 I took my degree **de** Doctor **de** Medicine **de la** University **de** London, and proceeded **a** Netley to go through the course prescribed for surgeons **en** the army. Having completed my studies there, I **era** duly attached **al** Fifth Northumberland Fusiliers as Assistant Surgeon. The regiment **era** stationed **en** India at the time, and before I could join it, the second Afghan war had broken out. On landing at Bombay, I learned that my corps had advanced through the passes, and **era** already deep **en** the enemy's country. I followed, however, with many other officers who were **en** the same situation as myself, and succeeded **en** reaching Candahar **en** safety, where I found my regiment, and at once entered upon my new duties.

The campaign brought honours and promotion **para** many, but for me **eso** had nothing but misfortune and disaster. I **era** removed **de** my brigade and attached **al** Berkshires, with whom I served at the fatal battle **de** Maiwand. There I **era** struck on the shoulder by a Jezail bullet, which shattered the bone and grazed the subclavian artery. I should have fallen into the hands **de los** murderous Ghazis had it not been for the devotion and courage shown by Murray, my orderly, who threw me across a pack - horse, and succeeded **en** bringing me safely **a las** British lines.

1

Worn with pain, and weak **desde el** prolonged hardships which I had undergone, I **era** removed, with a great train **de** wounded sufferers, **hacia** the base hospital at Peshawar. Here I rallied, and had already improved so far as to be able to walk about the wards, and even to bask a little upon the verandah, when I **era** struck down by enteric fever, that curse **de** our Indian possessions. For months my life **era** despaired of, and when at last I came to myself and became convalescent, I **estaba** so weak and emaciated that a medical board determined that not a day should be lost **en** sending me back **a** England. I **fui** dispatched, accordingly, **en** the troopship "Orontes," and landed a month later on Portsmouth jetty, with my health irretrievably ruined, but with permission **de una** paternal government to spend the next nine months **en** attempting to improve it.

I had neither kith nor kin **en** England, and **era** therefore as free as air -- or as free as an income **de** eleven shillings and sixpence a day will permit a man to be. Under such circumstances, I naturally gravitated **hacia** London, that great cesspool into which all the loungers and idlers **de el** Empire are irresistibly drained. There I stayed for some time at a private hotel **en** the Strand, leading a comfortless, meaningless existence, and spending such money as I had, considerably more freely than I ought. So alarming did the state **de** my finances become, that I soon realized that I must either leave the metropolis and rusticate somewhere **en** the country, or that I must make a complete alteration **en** my style **de** living. Choosing the latter alternative, I began by making up my mind to leave the hotel, and to take up my quarters **en** some less pretentious and less expensive domicile.

On the very day that I had come **a** this conclusion, I was standing at the Criterion Bar, when some one tapped me on the shoulder, and turning round I recognized young Stamford, who had been a dresser under me at Barts. The sight **de una** friendly face **en** the great wilderness **de** London is a pleasant thing indeed **para un** lonely man. **En** old days Stamford had never been a particular crony **de** mine, but now I hailed him with enthusiasm, and he, **en** his turn, appeared to be delighted to see me. **En** the exuberance **de** my joy, I asked him to lunch with me at the Holborn, and we started off together **en** a hansom.

"Whatever have **tú** been doing with yourself, Watson?" he asked **en** undisguised wonder, as we rattled through the crowded London streets. "**Tú** are as thin as a lath and as brown as a nut."

I gave him a short sketch **de** my adventures, and had hardly concluded it by the time that we reached our destination.

"Poor devil!" he said, commiseratingly, after he had listened **a** my misfortunes. "What are **tú** up to now?"

"Looking for lodgings." [3] I answered. "Trying to solve the problem as to whether it is possible to get comfortable rooms at a reasonable price."

"**Eso** has a strange thing," remarked my companion; "**tú** are the second man to - day **eso** has used that expression **para** me."

"And who **era** the first?" I asked.

"A fellow who is working at the chemical laboratory up at the hospital. He was bemoaning himself this morning **porque** he could not get someone to go halves with him **en** some nice rooms which he had found, and which were too much for his purse."

"By Jove!" I cried, "if he really wants someone to share the rooms and the expense, I am the very man for him. I should prefer having a partner to being alone."

Young Stamford looked rather strangely at me over his wine - glass. "**Tú** don't know Sherlock Holmes yet," he said; "perhaps **tú** would not care for him as a constant companion."

"Why, what is there against him?"

"Oh, I did not say **había** anything against him. He is a little queer **en** his ideas -- an enthusiast **en** some branches **de** science. As far as I know he is a decent fellow enough."

"A medical student, I suppose?" said I.

"No -- i have no idea what he intends to go in for. I believe he is well up **en** anatomy, and he is a first - class chemist; but, as far as I know, he has never taken out any systematic medical classes. His studies are very desultory and eccentric, but he has amassed a lot of out - of - the way knowledge which would astonish his professors."

"Did **tú** never ask him what he was going in for?" I asked.

"No; he is not a man that **eso** is easy to draw out, though he can be communicative enough when the fancy seizes him."

"I should like to meet him," I said. "If I am to lodge with anyone, I should prefer a man **de** studious and quiet habits. I am not strong enough yet to stand much noise or excitement. I had enough **de** both **en** Afghanistan to last me for the remainder **de** my natural existence. How could I meet this friend of yours?"

"He is sure to be at the laboratory," returned my companion. "He either avoids the place for weeks, or else he works there **desde** morning **hasta** night. If **tú** like, we shall drive round together after luncheon."

"Certainly," I answered, and the conversation drifted away into other channels.

3

As we made our way **hacia** the hospital after leaving the Holborn, Stamford gave me **unos pocos** more particulars about **el caballero** whom I proposed to take as a fellow - lodger.

"**Tú** mustn't blame me if **tú** don't get on with him," he said; "I know nothing more **de él** than I have learned **de** meeting him occasionally **en** the laboratory. **Tú** proposed this arrangement, so **tú** must not hold me responsible."

"If we don't get on **eso** will be easy to part company," I answered. "**Eso** seems **para** me, Stamford," I added, looking hard at my companion, "that **tú** have some reason for washing your hands **de** the matter. Is this fellow's temper so formidable, or what is **eso**? Don't be mealy - mouthed about it."

"It is not easy to express the inexpressible," he answered with a laugh. "Holmes is a little too scientific for my tastes -- **eso** approaches **hacia** cold - bloodedness. I could imagine his giving a friend a little pinch **del** latest vegetable alkaloid, not out **de** malevolence, **tú** understand, but simply out **de** a spirit **de** inquiry **en** order to have an accurate idea **de** the effects. To do him justice, I think that he would take **eso** himself with the same readiness. He appears to have a passion for definite and exact knowledge."

"Very right too."

"Yes, but **eso** may be pushed **hacia** excess. When it comes to beating the subjects **en** the dissecting - rooms with a stick, **eso** is certainly taking rather a bizarre shape."

"Beating the subjects!"

"Yes, to verify how far bruises may be produced after death. I saw him at it with my own eyes."

"And yet **tú** say he is not a medical student?"

"No. Heaven knows what the objects **de** his studies are. But here we are, and **tú** must form your own impressions about him." As he spoke, we turned down a narrow lane and passed through a small side - door, which opened into a wing **del** great hospital. **Era** familiar ground **para** me, and I needed no guiding as we ascended the bleak stone staircase and made our way down the long corridor with its vista **de** whitewashed wall and dun - coloured doors. Near the further end a low arched passage branched away **de eso** and led **hacia** the chemical laboratory.

This **era** a lofty chamber, lined and littered with countless bottles. Broad, low tables were scattered about, which bristled with retorts, test - tubes, and little Bunsen lamps, with their blue flickering flames. **Había** only one student **en** the room, who was bending over a distant table absorbed **en** his work. At the sound **de** our **pasos** he glanced round and sprang **a** his feet with a cry **de** pleasure. "I have found it! I have found it," he shouted **para** my companion, running towards us with a test - tube **en** his hand. "I have found a re - agent which is precipitated by hoemoglobin, [4] and by nothing else." Had he discovered a gold mine, greater delight could not have shone upon his features.

"Dr. Watson, Mr. Sherlock Holmes," said Stamford, introducing us.

"How are **tú**?" he said cordially, gripping my hand with a strength for which I should hardly have given him credit. "**Tú** have been **en** Afghanistan, I perceive."

"How on earth did **tú** know that?" I asked **en** astonishment.

"Never mind," said he, chuckling **para** himself. "The question now is about hoemoglobin. No doubt **tú** see the significance **de** this discovery of mine?"

"**Eso** is interesting, chemically, no doubt," I answered, "but practically----"

"Why, man, it is the most practical medico - legal discovery for years. Don't **tú** see that **eso** gives us an infallible test for blood stains. Come over here now!" He seized me by the coat - sleeve **en** his eagerness, and drew me over **hacia** the table at which he had been working. "Let us have some fresh blood," he said, digging a long bodkin into his finger, and drawing off the resulting drop **de** blood **en** a chemical pipette. "Now, I add this small quantity **de** blood **a** a litre **de** water. **Tú** perceive that the resulting mixture has the appearance **de** pure water. The proportion **de** blood can not be more than one **en** a million. I have no doubt, however, that we shall be able to obtain the characteristic reaction." As he spoke, he threw into the vessel **unos pocos** white crystals, and then added some drops **de un** transparent fluid. **En** an **instante** the contents assumed a dull mahogany colour, and a brownish dust was precipitated **a** the bottom **de** the glass jar.

"Ha! ha!" he cried, clapping his hands, and looking as delighted as a child with a new toy. "What do **tú** think **de eso**?"

"**Eso** seems to be a very delicate test," I remarked.

"Beautiful! beautiful! The old Guiacum test **era** very clumsy and uncertain. So is the microscopic examination for blood corpuscles. The latter is valueless if the stains are **unas pocas** hours old. Now, this appears to act as well whether the blood is old or new. Had this test been invented, there are hundreds **de** men now walking the earth who would long ago have paid the penalty **de** their crimes."

"Indeed!" I murmured.

"Criminal cases are continually hinging upon that one point. A man is suspected **de** a crime months perhaps after it has been committed. His linen or clothes are examined, and brownish stains discovered upon them. Are they blood stains, or mud stains, or rust stains, or fruit stains, or what are they? <u>**Esa**</u> is a question which has puzzled many an expert, and why? **Porque había** no reliable test. Now we have the Sherlock Holmes' test, and there will no longer be any difficulty."

His eyes fairly glittered as he spoke, and he put his hand over his heart and bowed as if to some applauding crowd conjured up by his imagination.

"**Tú** are to be congratulated," I remarked, considerably surprised at his enthusiasm.

"There was the case **de** Von Bischoff at Frankfort last year. He would certainly have been hung had this test been **en** existence. Then there was Mason **de** Bradford, and the notorious Muller, and Lefevre **de** Montpellier, and Samson **de** New Orleans. I could name a score **de** cases **en** which it would have been decisive."

"**Tú** seem to be a walking calendar **de** crime," said Stamford with a laugh. "**Tú** might start a paper on those lines. Call it the 'PoliceNews **del** Past.'"

"Very interesting reading it might be made, too," remarked Sherlock Holmes, sticking a small piece **de** plaster over the prick on his finger. "I have to be careful," he continued, turning **hacia** me with a smile, "for I dabble with poisons a good deal." He held out his hand as he spoke, and I noticed that **eso era** all mottled over with similar pieces **de** plaster, and discoloured with strong acids.

"We came here on business," said Stamford, sitting down on a high three - legged stool, and pushing another one **en** my direction with his foot. "My friend here wants to take diggings, and as <u>**vosotros**</u> were complaining that **tú** could get no one to go halves with you, I thought that I had better bring you together."

Sherlock Holmes seemed delighted at the idea **de** sharing his rooms with me. "I have my eye on a suite **en** Baker Street," he said, "which would suit us down to the ground. **Tú** don't mind the smell **de** strong tobacco, I hope?"

"I always smoke 'ship's'myself," I answered.

"**Eso** is good enough. I generally have chemicals about, and occasionally do experiments. Would **eso** annoy you?"

"By no means."

"Let me see -- what are my other shortcomings. I get **en** the dumps at times, and don't open my mouth for days on end. **Tú** must not think I am sulky when I do that. Just let me alone, and I will soon be right. What have **tú** to confess now? **Eso** is just as well for two fellows to know the worst **de** one another before they begin to live together."

I laughed at this cross - examination. "I keep a bull pup," I said, "and I object to rows **porque** my nerves are shaken, and I get up at all sorts **de** ungodly hours, and I am extremely lazy. I have another set **de** vices when I am well, but those are the principal ones at present."

"Do **tú** include violin - playing **en** your category **de** rows?" he asked, anxiously.

"**Eso** depends on the player," I answered. "A well - played violin is a treat for the gods -- a badly - played one----"

"Oh, **eso** is all right," he cried, with a merry laugh. "I think we may consider the thing as settled -- that is, if the rooms are agreeable to you."

"When shall we see them?"

"Call for me here at noon tomorrow, and we will go together and settle everything," he answered.

"All right -- noon exactly," said I, shaking his hand.

We left him working among his chemicals, and we walked together towards my hotel.

"By the way," I asked suddenly, stopping and turning upon Stamford, "how the deuce did he know that I had come **desde** Afghanistan?"

My companion smiled an enigmatical smile. "**Eso** has just his little peculiarity," he said. "A good many people have wanted to know how he finds <u>cosas</u> out."

"Oh! a mystery is **eso**?" I cried, rubbing my hands. "This is very piquant. I am much obliged **para** you for bringing us together. 'Theproper study **de** mankind is man,' **tú** know."

"**Tú** must study him, then," Stamford said, as he bade me good - bye. "**Tú** will find him a knotty problem, though. I will wager he learns more about you than **tú** about him. Good - bye."

"Good - bye," I answered, and strolled on **hacia** my hotel, considerably interested **en** my new acquaintance.

weeve

Chapter 1

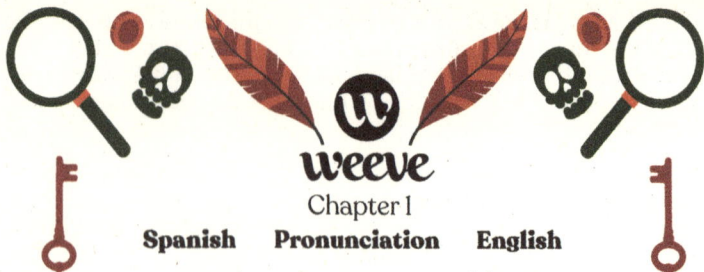

Spanish	Pronunciation	English
en	en	in
de	de	from
a	a	to
era	eɾa	was
al	al	to the
para	paɾa	to
eso	eso	it
hacia	asia	to
estaba	estaba	was
fui	fwi	was
tú	tu	you
porque	poɾke	because
había	abja	there was
hasta	asta	to
unos pocos	unos pokos	a few
del	del	of the
pasos	pasos	steps
instante	instante	instant

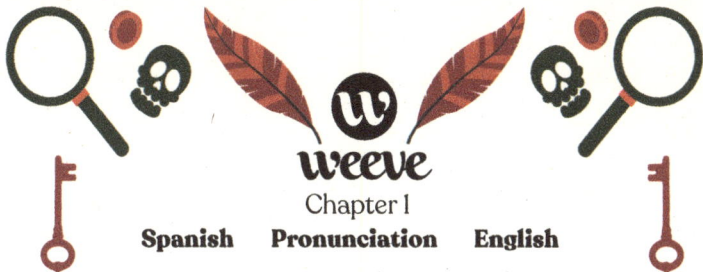

weeve
Chapter 1

Spanish	Pronunciation	English
unas pocas	unas pokas	a few
esa	esa	that
vosotros	bosotros	you
cosas	kosas	things

2

THE SCIENCE OF DEDUCTION

Weeve Reading Tip: If you struggle reading the weaved words try reading the full sentence and ignore the fact you didn't understand the foreign word. Your brain will subconsciously process this word, using context to better understand it for the next time it appears.

We met next day as he had arranged, and inspected the rooms at No. 221B, Baker Street, **de** which he had spoken at our meeting. They consisted of a couple **de** comfortable bedrooms and a single large airy sitting - room, cheerfully furnished, and illuminated by two broad windows. So desirable **en** every way were the apartments, and so moderate did the terms seem when divided between us, that the bargain **era** concluded upon the spot, and we at once entered into possession. That very evening I moved my **cosas** round **de** the hotel, and on the following morning Sherlock Holmes followed me with several boxes and portmanteaus. For a day or two we were busily employed **en** unpacking and laying out our property **al** best advantage. That done, we gradually began to settle down and to accommodate ourselves **para** our new surroundings.

Holmes **era** certainly not a difficult man to live with. He **era** quiet **en** his ways, and his habits were regular. **Era** rare for him to be up after ten at night, and he had invariably breakfasted and gone out before I rose **en** the morning. Sometimes he spent his day at the chemical laboratory, sometimes **en** the dissecting - rooms, and occasionally **en** long walks, which appeared to take him into the lowest portions **de la** City. Nothing could exceed his energy when the working fit **era** upon him; but now and again a reaction would seize him, and for days on end he would lie upon the sofa **en** the sitting - room, hardly uttering a word or moving a muscle **desde** morning **hasta** night. On these occasions I have noticed such a dreamy, vacant expression **en** his eyes, that I might have suspected him **de** being addicted **a** the use **de** some narcotic, had not the temperance and cleanliness **de** his whole life forbidden such a notion.

As the weeks went by, my interest **en** him and my curiosity as to his aims **en** life, gradually deepened and increased. His very person and appearance were such as to strike the attention **del** most casual observer. **En** height he **era** rather over six **pies**, and so excessively lean that he seemed to be considerably taller. His eyes were sharp and piercing, save during those intervals **de** torpor to which I have alluded; and his thin, hawk - like nose gave his whole expression an air **de** alertness and decision. His chin, too, had the prominence and squareness which mark the man **de** determination. His hands were invariably blotted with ink and stained with chemicals, yet he **era** possessed **de** extraordinary delicacy **de** touch, as I frequently had occasion to observe when I watched him manipulating his fragile philosophical instruments.

The reader may set me down as a hopeless busybody, when I confess how much this man stimulated my curiosity, and how often I endeavoured to break through the reticence which he showed on all **eso** concerned himself. Before pronouncing judgment, however, be it remembered, how objectless **era** my life, and how little **había** to engage my attention. My health forbade me **de** venturing out unless the weather **era** exceptionally genial, and I had no friends who would call upon me and break the monotony **de** my daily existence. Under these circumstances, I eagerly hailed the little mystery which hung around my companion, and spent much **de** my time **en** endeavouring to unravel **eso**.

He was not studying medicine. He had himself, **en** reply **a** a question, confirmed Stamford's opinion upon that point. Neither did he appear to have pursued any course **de** reading which might fit him for a degree **en** science or any other recognized portal which would give him an entrance into the learned **mundo**. Yet his zeal for certain studies **era** remarkable, and within eccentric limits his knowledge **era** so extraordinarily ample and minute that his observations have fairly astounded me. Surely no man would work so hard or attain such precise information unless he had some definite end **en** view. Desultory readers are seldom remarkable for the exactness **de sus** learning. No man burdens his mind with small matters unless he has some very good reason for doing so.

His ignorance **era** as remarkable as his knowledge. **De** contemporary literature, philosophy and politics he appeared to know next to nothing. Upon my quoting Thomas Carlyle, he inquired **en** the naivest way who he might be and what he had done. My surprise reached a climax, however, when I found incidentally that he **era** ignorant **de la** Copernican Theory and **de** the composition **del** Solar System. That any civilized human being **en** this nineteenth century should not be aware that the earth travelled round the sun appeared to be **para** me such an extraordinary fact that I could hardly realize it.

"**Tú** appear to be astonished," he said, smiling at my expression **de** surprise. "Now that I do know **eso** I shall do my best to forget **eso**."

"To forget **eso**!"

"**Tú** see," he explained, "I consider that a man's brain originally is like a little empty attic, and **tú** have to stock it with such furniture as **tú** choose. A fool takes **en** all the lumber **de** every sort that he comes across, so that the knowledge which might be useful **para** him gets crowded out, or at best is jumbled up with a lot **de** other **cosas** so that he has a difficulty **en** laying his hands upon **eso**. Now the skilful workman is very careful indeed as **para** what he takes into his brain - attic. He will have nothing but the tools which may help him **en** doing his work, but **de** these he has a large assortment, and all **en** the most perfect order. It is a mistake to think that that little room has elastic walls and can distend **a** any extent. Depend upon it there comes a time when for every addition **de** knowledge **tú** forget something that **tú** knew before. **Eso** is **de la** highest importance, therefore, not to have useless facts elbowing out the useful ones."

"But the Solar System!" I protested.

"What the deuce is it **para** me?" he interrupted impatiently; "**tú** say that we **ir** round the sun. If we went round the moon **eso** would not make a pennyworth **de** difference **para** me or **para** my work."

I **era** on the point **de** asking him what that work might be, but something **en** his manner showed me that the question would be an unwelcome one. I pondered over our short conversation, however, and endeavoured to draw my deductions **de eso**. He said that he would acquire no knowledge which did not bear upon his object. Therefore all the knowledge which he possessed **era** such as would be useful **para** him. I enumerated **en** my own mind all the various points upon which he had shown me that he **era** exceptionally well - informed. I **incluso** took a pencil and jotted them down. I could not help smiling at the document when I had completed it. It ran **en** this way--

Sherlock Holmes -- his limits.

1. Knowledge **de** Literature.--Nil.

2. Philosophy.--Nil.

3. Astronomy.--Nil.

4. Politics.--Feeble.

5. Botany.--Variable. Well up **en** belladonna, opium, and poisons generally. Knows nothing **de** practical gardening.

6. Geology.--Practical, but limited. Tells at a glance different soils **de** each other. After walks has shown me splashes upon his trousers, and told me by their colour and consistence **en** what part **de** London he had received them.

7. Chemistry.--Profound.

8. Anatomy.--Accurate, but unsystematic.

9. Sensational Literature.--Immense. He appears to know every detail **de** every horror perpetrated **en** the century.

10. Plays the violin well.

11. Is an expert singlestick player, boxer, and swordsman.

12. Has a good practical knowledge **de** British law.

When I had got so far **en** my list I threw it into the fire **en** despair. "If I can only find what **el compañero** is driving at by reconciling all these accomplishments, and discovering a calling which needs them all," I said **para** myself, "I may as well give up the attempt at once."

I see that I have alluded above to his powers upon the violin. These were very remarkable, but as eccentric as all his other accomplishments. That he could play pieces, and difficult pieces, I knew well, **porque** at my request he has played me some **de** Mendelssohn's Lieder, and other favourites. When left **para** himself, however, he would seldom produce any music or attempt any recognized air. Leaning back **en** his arm - chair **de** an evening, he would close his eyes and scrape carelessly at the fiddle which **era** thrown across his knee. Sometimes the chords were sonorous and melancholy. Occasionally they were fantastic and cheerful. Clearly they reflected the thoughts which possessed him, but whether the music aided those thoughts, or whether the playing **era** simply the result **de** a whim or fancy **era** more than I could determine. I might have rebelled against these exasperating solos had it not been that he usually terminated them by playing **en** quick succession a whole series **de** my favourite airs as a slight compensation for the trial upon my patience.

During the **primera** week or so we had no callers, and I had begun to think that my companion **era** as friendless a man as I **era** myself. Presently, however, I found that he had many acquaintances, and those **en** the most different classes **de** society. There **era** one little sallow rat - faced, dark - eyed **compañero** who **era** introduced **para** me as Mr. Lestrade, and who came three or four times **en** a single week. One morning a young girl called, fashionably dressed, and stayed for half an hour or more. The same afternoon brought a grey - headed, seedy visitor, looking like a Jew pedlar, who appeared **para** me to be much excited, and who **era** closely followed by a slip - shod elderly woman. On **otra** occasion an old white - haired **caballero** had an interview with my companion; and on **otra** a railway porter **en** his velveteen uniform. When any **de** these nondescript individuals put **en** an appearance, Sherlock Holmes used to beg for the use **de** the sitting - room, and I would retire **a** my bed - room. He always apologized to me for putting me to this inconvenience. "I have to use this room as a place **de** business," he said, "and these people are my clients." Again I had an opportunity **de** asking him a point blank question, and again my delicacy prevented me **de** forcing **otro** man to confide **en** me. I imagined at the time that he had some strong reason for not alluding **a eso**, but he soon dispelled the idea by coming round **a** the subject **de** his own accord.

Era upon the 4th **de** March, as I have good reason to remember, that I rose somewhat earlier than usual, and found that Sherlock Holmes had not yet finished his breakfast. The landlady had become so accustomed **a** my late habits that my place had not been laid nor my coffee prepared. With the unreasonable petulance **de** mankind I rang the bell and gave a curt intimation that I **era** ready. Then I picked up a magazine **de** the table and attempted to while away the time with **eso**, while my companion munched silently at his toast. One **de** the articles had a pencil mark at the heading, and I naturally began to run my eye through **eso**.

Its somewhat ambitious title **era** "The Book **de** Life," and **eso** attempted to show how much an observant man might learn by an accurate and systematic examination **de** all that came **en** his way. **Eso** struck me as being a remarkable mixture **de** shrewdness and **de** absurdity. The reasoning **era** close and intense, but the deductions appeared **para** me to be far - fetched and exaggerated. The writer claimed by a momentary expression, a twitch **de** a muscle or a glance **de** an eye, to fathom a man's inmost thoughts. Deceit, according **para** him, was an impossibility **en** the case **de** one trained to observation and analysis. His conclusions were as infallible as so many propositions **de** Euclid. So startling would his results appear **al** uninitiated that until they learned the processes by which he had arrived at them they might well consider him as a necromancer.

"**Desde** a drop **de** water," said the writer, "a logician could infer the possibility **de** an Atlantic or a Niagara without having seen or

14

heard **de** one or the other. So all life is a great chain, the nature **de** which is known whenever we are shown a single link **de eso**. Like all other arts, the Science **de** Deduction and Analysis is one which can only be acquired by long and patient study nor is life long enough to allow any mortal to attain the highest possible perfection **en eso**. Before turning **a** those moral and mental aspects **de** the matter which present the greatest difficulties, let the enquirer begin by mastering more elementary problems. Let him, on meeting **un compañero** - mortal, learn at a glance to distinguish the history **de** the man, and the trade or profession to which he belongs. Puerile as such an exercise may seem, **eso** sharpens the faculties **de** observation, and teaches one where to look and what to look for. By a man's finger nails, by his coat - sleeve, by his boot, by his trouser knees, by the callosities **de** his forefinger and thumb, by his expression, by his shirt cuffs -- by each **de** these **cosas** a man's calling is plainly revealed. That all united should fail to enlighten the competent enquirer **en** any case is almost inconceivable."

"What ineffable twaddle!" I cried, slapping the magazine down on the table, "I never read such rubbish **en** my life."

"What is **eso**?" asked Sherlock Holmes.

"Why, this article," I said, pointing at **él** with my egg spoon as I sat down to my breakfast. "I see that **tú** have read **eso** since **tú** have marked it. I don't deny that **eso** is smartly written. **Eso** irritates me though. **Eso** is evidently the theory **de** some arm - chair lounger who evolves all these neat little paradoxes **en** the seclusion **de** his own study. **Eso** is not practical. I should like to see him clapped down **en** a third class carriage on the Underground, and asked to give the trades **de** all his **compañero** - travellers. I would lay a thousand to one against him."

"**Tú** would lose your money," Sherlock Holmes remarked calmly. "As for the article I wrote it myself."

" **Tú!**"

"Yes, I have a turn both for observation and for deduction. The theories which I have expressed there, and which appear **para** you to be so chimerical are really extremely practical -- so practical that I depend upon them for my bread and cheese."

"And how?" I asked involuntarily.

"Well, I have a trade **de** my own. I suppose I am the only one **en el mundo**. I am a consulting detective, if **tú** can understand what **eso** is. Here **en** London we have lots **de** Government detectives and lots **de** private ones. When these fellows are at fault they come **a** me, and I manage to put them on the right scent. They lay all the evidence before me, and I am generally able, by the help

de my knowledge **de** the history **del crimen**, to set them straight. There is a strong family resemblance about misdeeds, and if **tú** have all the details **de un** thousand at your finger ends, **eso** is odd if **tú** can't unravel the thousand and **primero**. Lestrade is a well - known detective. He got himself into a fog recently over a forgery case, and **eso fue** what brought him here."

"And these other people?"

"They are mostly sent on by private inquiry agencies. They are all people who are **en** trouble about something, and want a little enlightening. I listen **a** their story, they listen **a** my comments, and then I pocket my fee."

"But do **tú** mean to say," I said, "that without leaving your room **tú** can unravel some knot which other men can make nothing **de**, although they have seen every detail for themselves?"

"Quite so. I have a kind **de** intuition that way. Now and again a case turns up which is a little more complex. Then I have to bustle about and see **cosas** with my own eyes. **Tú** see I have a lot **de** special knowledge which I apply **a** the problem, and which facilitates matters wonderfully. Those rules **de** deduction laid down **en** that article which aroused your scorn, are invaluable **para** me **en** practical work. Observation with me is second nature. **Tú** appeared to be surprised when I told you, on our **primer** meeting, that **tú** had come **de** Afghanistan."

"You were told, no doubt."

"Nothing **de** the sort. I knew **tú** came **de** Afghanistan. From long habit the train **de** thoughts ran so swiftly through my mind, that I arrived at the conclusion without being conscious **de** intermediate **pasos**. There were such **pasos**, however. The train **de** reasoning ran, 'Hereis **un caballero de un** medical type, but with the air **de un** military man. Clearly an army doctor, then. He has just come **de** the tropics, for his face is dark, and **eso** is not the natural tint **de** his skin, for his wrists are fair. He has undergone hardship and sickness, as his haggard face says clearly. His left arm has been injured. He holds it **en** a stiff and unnatural manner. Where **en** the tropics could an English army doctor have seen much hardship and got his arm wounded? Clearly **en** Afghanistan.' The whole train **de** thought did not occupy a second. I then remarked that **tú** came **de** Afghanistan, and **tú** were astonished."

"**Eso** is simple enough as **tú** explain **eso**," I said, smiling. "**Tú** remind me **de** Edgar Allen Poe's Dupin. I had no idea that such individuals did exist outside **de** stories."

Sherlock Holmes rose and lit his pipe. "No doubt **tú** think that **tú** are complimenting me **en** comparing me **a** Dupin," he observed. "Now, **en** my opinion, Dupin **era** a very inferior **compañero**.

That trick **de** his **de** breaking **en** on his friends' thoughts with an apropos remark after a quarter **de** an hour's silence is really very showy and superficial. He had some analytical genius, no doubt; but he **era** by no means such a phenomenon as Poe appeared to imagine."

"Have **tú** read Gaboriau's works?" I asked. "Does Lecoq come up **a** your idea **de** a detective?"

Sherlock Holmes sniffed sardonically. "Lecoq **era** a miserable bungler," he said, **en** an angry voice; "he had only one thing to recommend him, and **eso era** his energy. That book made me positively ill. The question **era** how to identify an unknown prisoner. I could have done **eso en** twenty - four hours. Lecoq took six months or so. It might be made a text - book for detectives to teach them what to avoid."

I felt rather indignant at having two characters whom I had admired treated **en** this cavalier style. I walked over **hacia** the window, and stood looking out into the busy street. "This **compañero** may be very clever," I said **para** myself, "but he is certainly very conceited."

"There are no crimes and no criminals **en** these days," he said, querulously. "What is the use **de** having brains **en** our profession. I know well that I have **eso en** me to make my name famous. No man lives or has ever lived who has brought the same amount **de** study and **de** natural talent **para** the detection **del crimen** which I have done. And what is the result? There is no **crimen** to detect, or, at most, some bungling villainy with a motive so transparent that **incluso** a Scotland Yard official can see through **eso**."

I **era** still annoyed at his bumptious style **de** conversation. I thought it best to change the topic.

"I wonder what **ese tipo** is looking for?" I asked, pointing **para** a stalwart, plainly - dressed individual who was walking slowly down the other side **de** the street, looking anxiously at the numbers. He had a large blue envelope **en** his hand, and **era** evidently the bearer **de** a message.

"**Tú** mean the retired sergeant **de** Marines," said Sherlock Holmes.

"Brag and bounce!" thought I **para** myself. "He knows that I can not verify his guess."

The thought had hardly passed through my mind when the man whom we were watching caught sight **de** the number on our door, and ran rapidly across the roadway. We heard a loud knock, a deep voice below, and heavy **pasos** ascending the stair.

"For Mr. Sherlock Holmes," he said, stepping into the room and handing my friend the letter.

Here **era** an opportunity **de** taking the conceit out **de él**. He little thought **de** this when he made that random shot. "May I ask, my lad," I said, **en** the blandest voice, "what your trade may be?"

"Commissionaire, sir," he said, gruffly. "Uniform away for repairs."

"And **tú** were?" I asked, with a slightly malicious glance at my companion.

"A sergeant, sir, Royal Marine Light Infantry, sir. No answer? Right, sir."

He clicked his heels together, raised his hand **en** a salute, and **era** gone.

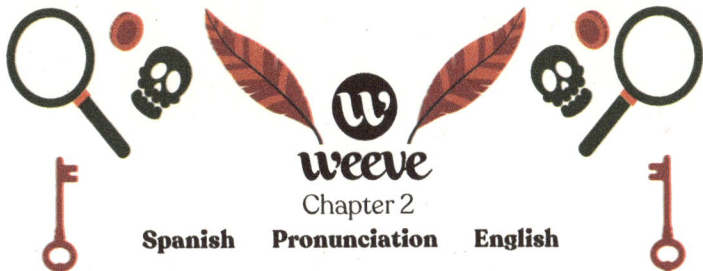

Spanish	Pronunciation	English
pies	pjes	feet
mundo	mundo	world
ir	ir	go
incluso	inkluso	even
primera	primera	first
otra	otra	another
otro	otro	another
primero	primero	first
primer	primer	first
ese tipo	ese tipo	that fellow

3

THE LAURISTAN GARDEN MYSTERY

<u>**Yo**</u> Confess that **era** considerably startled by this fresh proof **del** practical nature **de** my companion's theories. My respect for <u>**su**</u> powers **de** analysis increased wondrously. There still remained some lurking suspicion **en** my mind, <u>**sin embargo**</u>, that the whole thing **era** a pre - arranged episode, intended to dazzle me, though what earthly object he could have **en** taking me in **era** past my comprehension. When **yo** looked at him he had finished reading the note, and **sus** eyes had assumed the vacant, lack - lustre expression which showed mental abstraction.

"How **en el mundo** did **tú** deduce that?" **Yo** asked.

"Deduce what?" said he, petulantly.

"Why, that he **era** a retired sergeant **de** Marines."

"**Yo** have no time for trifles," he answered, brusquely; then with a smile, "Excuse my rudeness. <u>**You**</u> broke the thread **de** my thoughts; but perhaps it is as well. So **tú** actually were not able to see that that man **era** a sergeant **de** Marines?"

"No, indeed."

"**Era** easier to know **eso** than to explain why **yo** knew **eso**. If **tú** were asked to prove that two and two made four, <u>**podrías**</u> find some difficulty, and yet **tú** are quite sure **de** the fact. **Incluso**
20

across the street **yo** could see a great blue anchor tattooed on the back **del** fellow's hand. **Eso** smacked **de** the sea. He had a military carriage, **sin embargo**, and regulation side whiskers. There we have the marine. He **era** a man with some amount **de** self - importance and a certain air **de** command. **Tú** must have observed the way **en** which he held **su** head and swung **su** cane. A steady, respectable, middle - aged man, too, on the face **de él** -- all facts which led me to believe that he had been a sergeant."

"Wonderful!" **Yo** ejaculated.

"Commonplace," said Holmes, though **yo** thought **de su** expression that he **era** pleased at my evident surprise and admiration. "**Yo** said just now that there were no criminals. It appears that **yo** am wrong -- look at this!" He threw me over the note which the commissionaire had brought.

"Why," **yo** cried, as **yo** cast my eye over **eso**, "this is terrible!"

"**Eso** does seem to be a little out **del** common," he remarked, calmly. "Would **tú** mind reading it **para** me aloud?"

This is the letter which **yo** read to him----

"My Dear Mr. Sherlock Holmes, --

"There has been a bad business during the night at 3, Lauriston Gardens, off the Brixton Road. Our man on the beat saw a light there about two **en** the morning, and as the house **era** an empty one, suspected that something **era** amiss. He found the door open, and **en** the front room, which is bare **de** furniture, discovered the body **de un caballero**, well dressed, and having cards **en su bolsillo** bearing the name **de** 'EnochJ. Drebber, Cleveland, Ohio, **Tú**.S.A.' There had been no robbery, nor is there any evidence as to how the man met **su** death. There are marks **de** blood **en** the room, but there is no wound upon **su** person. We are at a loss as to how he came into the empty house; indeed, the whole affair is a puzzler. If **tú** can come round **a** the house any time before twelve, **tú** will find me there. **Yo** have left everything **en** statu quo until **yo** hear **de ti**. If **tú** are unable to come **yo** shall give you fuller details, and would esteem it a great kindness if **tú** would favour me with your opinion. Yours faithfully,

"Tobias Gregson."

"Gregson is the smartest **de** the Scotland Yarders," my friend remarked; "he and Lestrade are the pick **de un** bad lot. They are both quick and energetic, but conventional -- shockingly so. They have **su** knives into one **otro**, too. They are as jealous as a pair **de** professional beauties. There will be some fun over this case if they are both put upon the scent."

Yo estaba amazed at the calm way **en** which he rippled on.

"Surely there is not a moment to be lost," **yo** cried, "shall **ir** and order you a cab?"

"**Yo** am not sure about whether **yo** shall **ir**. **Yo** am the most incurably lazy devil **que** ever stood **en** shoe leather -- that is, when the fit is on me, for **yo** can be spry enough at times."

"Why, **eso** is just such a chance as **tú** have been longing for."

"My dear **compañero**, what does **eso** matter **para** me. Supposing **yo** unravel the whole matter, **tú** may be sure that Gregson, Lestrade, and Co. will pocket all the credit. **Eso** comes **de** being an unofficial personage."

"But he begs you to **ayudar** him."

"Yes. He knows that **yo** am **su** superior, and acknowledges **eso** **para** me; but he would cut **su** tongue out before he would own it **a** any third person. **Sin embargo**, we may as well **ir** and have a look. **Yo** shall work it out on my own hook. **Yo** may have a laugh at them if **yo** have nothing else. Come on!"

He hustled on **su** overcoat, and bustled about **en** a way **que** showed that an energetic fit had superseded the apathetic one.

"Get your hat," he said.

"**Tú** wish me to come?"

"Yes, if **tú** have nothing better to do." A minute later we were both **en** a hansom, driving furiously for the Brixton Road.

Era a foggy, cloudy morning, and a dun - coloured veil hung over the house - tops, looking like the reflection **de** the mud - coloured streets beneath. My companion **era en** the **mejor** **de** spirits, and prattled away about Cremona fiddles, and the difference between a Stradivarius and an Amati. As for myself, **yo estaba** silent, for the dull weather and the melancholy business upon which we were engaged, depressed my spirits.

"**Tú** don't seem to give much thought **a** the matter **en** hand," **yo** said at last, interrupting Holmes' musical disquisition.

"No data yet," he answered. It is a capital mistake to theorize before **tú** have all the evidence. **Eso** biases the judgment."

"**Tú** will have your data soon," **yo** remarked, pointing with my finger; "this is the Brixton Road, and **esa** is the house, if **yo** am not very much mistaken."

"So it is. Stop, driver, stop!" We were still a hundred yards or so **de** it, but he insisted upon our alighting, and we finished our journey upon foot.

Number 3, Lauriston Gardens wore an ill - omened and minatory look. **Era** one **de** four which stood back some little way **de** the street, two being occupied and two empty. The latter looked out with three tiers **de** vacant melancholy windows, which were blank and dreary, save that here and there a "To Let" card had developed like a cataract upon the bleared panes. A small garden sprinkled over with a scattered eruption **de** sickly plants separated each **de** these houses **de** the street, and **era** traversed by a narrow pathway, yellowish **en** colour, and consisting apparently **de** a mixture **de** clay and **de** gravel. The whole place **era** very sloppy **de** the rain which had fallen through the night. The garden **era** bounded by a three - foot brick wall with a fringe **de** wood rails upon the top, and against this wall was leaning a stalwart police constable, surrounded by a small knot **de** loafers, who craned **sus** necks and strained **sus** eyes **en** the vain hope **de** catching some glimpse **de** the proceedings within.

Yo had imagined that Sherlock Holmes would at once have hurried into the house and plunged into a study **del misterio**. Nothing appeared to be further **de su** intention. With an air **de** nonchalance which, under the circumstances, seemed **para** me to border upon affectation, he lounged up and down the pavement, and gazed vacantly at the ground, the sky, the opposite houses and the line **de** railings. Having finished **su** scrutiny, he proceeded slowly down the path, or rather down the fringe **de** grass which flanked the path, keeping **sus** eyes riveted upon the ground. Twice he stopped, and once **yo** saw him smile, and heard him utter an exclamation **de** satisfaction. There were many marks **de** footsteps upon the wet clayey soil, but since the police had been coming and going over it, **yo era** unable to see how my companion could hope to learn anything **de eso**. Still **yo** had had such extraordinary evidence **de** the quickness **de sus** perceptive faculties, that **yo** had no doubt that he could see a great deal which **era** hidden **de** me.

At the door **de** the house we were met by a tall, white - faced, flaxen - haired man, with a notebook **en su** hand, who rushed forward and wrung my companion's hand with effusion. "It is indeed kind **de tú** to come," he said, "**yo** have had everything left untouched."

"Except that!" my friend answered, pointing at the pathway. "If a herd **de** buffaloes had passed along there could not be a greater mess. No doubt, **sin embargo, tú** had drawn your own conclusions, Gregson, before **tú** permitted this."

"**Yo** have had so much to do inside the house," the detective said evasively. "My colleague, Mr. Lestrade, is here. **Yo** had relied upon him to look after this."

Holmes glanced at me and raised **sus** eyebrows sardonically. "With two such men as yourself and Lestrade upon the ground, there will not be much for a third party to find out," he said.

Gregson rubbed **sus** hands **en** a self - satisfied way. "**Yo** think we have done all that can be done," he answered; "it is a queer case though, and **yo** knew your taste for such **cosas**."

"**Tú** did not come here **en** a cab?" asked Sherlock Holmes.

"No, sir."

"Nor Lestrade?"

"No, sir."

"Then let us **ir** and look at the room." With which inconsequent remark he strode on into the house, followed by Gregson, whose features expressed **su** astonishment.

A short passage, bare planked and dusty, led **hacia** the kitchen and offices. Two doors opened out **de** it **hacia** the left and **hacia** the right. One **de** these had obviously been closed for many weeks. The other belonged **a** the dining - room, which **era** the apartment **en** which the mysterious affair had occurred. Holmes walked in, and **yo** followed him with that subdued feeling at my heart which the presence **de** death inspires.

Era a large square room, looking all the larger **de** the absence **de** all furniture. A vulgar flaring paper adorned the walls, but **era** blotched **en** places with mildew, and here and there great strips had become detached and hung down, exposing the yellow plaster beneath. Opposite the door **era** a showy fireplace, surmounted by a mantelpiece **de** imitation white marble. On one corner **de** this **era** stuck the stump **de un** red wax candle. The solitary window **era** so dirty that the light **era** hazy and uncertain, giving a dull grey tinge **a** everything, which **era** intensified by the thick layer **de** dust which coated the whole apartment.

All these details **yo** observed afterwards. At present my attention **era** centred upon the single grim motionless figure which lay stretched upon the boards, with vacant sightless eyes staring up at the discoloured ceiling. **Era** that **de** a man about forty - three or forty - four years **de** age, middle - sized, broad shouldered, with crisp curling black hair, and a short stubbly beard. He **era** dressed **en** a heavy broadcloth frock coat and waistcoat, with light - coloured trousers, and immaculate collar and cuffs. A top hat, well brushed and trim, was placed upon the floor beside him. **Sus** hands were clenched and **sus** arms thrown abroad, while **sus** lower limbs were interlocked as though **su** death struggle had been a grievous one. On **su** rigid face there stood an expression **de** horror, and as **eso** seemed **para** me, **de** hatred, such as **yo** have never seen upon human features. This malignant and terrible contortion, combined with the low forehead, blunt nose, and prognathous jaw gave the dead man a singularly simious and ape

- like appearance, which **era** increased by **su** writhing, unnatural posture. **Yo** have seen death **en** many forms, but never has **eso** appeared **para** me **en** a more fearsome aspect than **en** that dark grimy apartment, which looked out upon one **del** main arteries **de** suburban London.

Lestrade, lean and ferret - like as ever, was standing by the doorway, and greeted my companion and myself.

"This case will make a stir, sir," he remarked. "It beats anything **yo** have seen, and **yo** am no chicken."

"There is no clue?" said Gregson.

"None at all," chimed **en** Lestrade.

Sherlock Holmes approached the body, and, kneeling down, examined it intently. "**Tú** are sure that there is no wound?" he asked, pointing **hacia** numerous gouts and splashes **de** blood which lay all round.

"Positive!" cried both detectives.

"Then, **por supuesto**, this blood belongs **a un** second individual-- presumably the murderer, if murder has been committed. **Eso** reminds me **de** the circumstances attendant on the death **de** Van Jansen, **en** Utrecht, **en** the year '34. Do **tú** remember the case, Gregson?"

"No, sir."

"Read it up -- **tú** really should. There is nothing new under the sun. **Eso** has all been done before."

As he spoke, **sus** nimble fingers were flying here, there, and everywhere, feeling, pressing, unbuttoning, examining, while **sus** eyes wore the same far - away expression which **yo** have already remarked upon. So swiftly **era** the examination made, that one would hardly have guessed the minuteness with which **era** conducted. Finally, he sniffed the dead man's lips, and then glanced at the soles **de sus** patent leather boots.

"He has not been moved at all?" he asked.

"No more than **era** necessary for the purposes **de** our examination."

"**Tú** can take him **a** the mortuary now," he said. "There is nothing more to be learned."

Gregson had a stretcher and four men at hand. At **su** call they entered the room, and the stranger **era** lifted and carried out. As they raised him, a ring tinkled down and rolled across the floor. Lestrade grabbed it up and stared at **eso** with mystified eyes.

"There has been a woman here," he cried. "It has a woman's wedding - ring."

He held it out, as he spoke, upon the palm **de su** hand. We all gathered round him and gazed at **eso**. There could be no doubt that that circlet **de** plain gold had once adorned the finger **de** a bride.

"This complicates matters," said Gregson. "Heaven knows, they were complicated enough before."

"**Tú** are sure **eso** doesn't simplify them?" observed Holmes. "There is nothing to be learned by staring at **eso**. What did **tú** find **en sus** pockets?"

"We have it all here," said Gregson, pointing **a** a litter **de** objects upon one **del** bottom **pasos de** the stairs. "A gold watch, No. 97163, by Barraud, **de** London. Gold Albert chain, very heavy and solid. Gold ring, with masonic device. Gold pin -- bull - dog's head, with rubies as eyes. Russian leather card - case, with cards **de** Enoch J. Drebber **de** Cleveland, corresponding with the E. J. D. upon the linen. No purse, but loose money **a** the extent **de** seven pounds thirteen. **Edición de bolsillo de** Boccaccio's 'Decameron,' with name **de** Joseph Stangerson upon the fly - leaf. Two letters -- one addressed **para** E. J. Drebber and one **para** Joseph Stangerson."

"At what address?"

"American Exchange, Strand -- to be left till called for. They are both **de el** Guion Steamship Company, and refer **a** the sailing **de sus** boats **de** Liverpool. It is clear that this unfortunate man **era** about to return **a** New York."

"Have **tú** made any inquiries as to this man, Stangerson?"

"**Yo** did **eso** at once, sir," said Gregson. "**Yo** have had advertisements sent **a** all the newspapers, and one **de** my men has gone **al** American Exchange, but he has not returned yet."

"Have **tú** sent **a** Cleveland?"

"We telegraphed this morning."

"How did **tú** word your inquiries?"

"We simply detailed the circumstances, and said that we should be glad **de** any information which could **ayudar** us."

"**Tú** did not ask for particulars on any point which appeared **para** you to be crucial?"

"**Yo** asked about Stangerson."

"Nothing else? Is there no circumstance on which this whole case appears to hinge? Will **tú** not telegraph again?"

"**Yo** have said all **yo** have to say," said Gregson, **en** an offended voice.

Sherlock Holmes chuckled **para** himself, and appeared to be about to make some remark, when Lestrade, who had been **en** the front room while we were holding this conversation **en** the hall, reappeared upon the scene, rubbing **sus** hands **en** a pompous and self - satisfied manner.

"Mr. Gregson," he said, "**yo** have just made a discovery **de la** highest importance, and one which would have been overlooked had **yo** not made a careful examination **de** the walls."

The little man's eyes sparkled as he spoke, and he **era** evidently **en** a state **de** suppressed exultation at having scored a point against **su** colleague.

"Come here," he said, bustling back into the room, the atmosphere **de** which felt clearer since the removal **de** its ghastly inmate. "Now, stand there!"

He struck a match on **su** boot and held it up against the wall.

"Look at that!" he said, triumphantly.

Yo have remarked that the paper had fallen away **en** parts. **En** this particular corner **de** the room a large piece had peeled off, leaving a yellow square **de** coarse plastering. Across this bare space there **era** scrawled **en** blood - red letters a single word--

Rache.

"What do **tú** think **de eso**?" cried the detective, with the air **de** a showman exhibiting **su** show. "This **era** overlooked **porque estaba en** the darkest corner **de** the room, and no one thought **de** looking there. The murderer has written it with **su** or her own blood. See this smear where **eso** has trickled down the wall! **Eso** disposes **de** the idea **de** suicide anyhow. Why was that corner chosen to write **eso** on? **Yo** will tell you. See that candle on the mantelpiece. **Era** lit at the time, and if **era** lit this corner would be the brightest instead **del** darkest portion **de** the wall."

"And what does **eso** mean now that **tú** have found **eso**?" asked Gregson **en** a depreciatory voice.

"Mean? Why, **eso** means that the writer was going to put the female name Rachel, but **fue** disturbed before he or she had time to finish. **Tú** mark my **palabras**, when this case comes to be cleared up **tú** will find that a woman named Rachel has something to do with **eso**. It is all very well for you to laugh, Mr. Sherlock Holmes. **Tú** may be very smart and clever, but the old hound is the **mejor**, when all is said and done."

"**Yo** really beg your pardon!" said my companion, who had ruffled the little man's temper by bursting into an explosion **de** laughter. "**Tú** certainly have the credit **de** being the **primero de** us to find this out, and, as **tú** say, **eso** bears every mark **de** having been written by the other participant **en** last night's **misterio**. **Yo** have not had time to examine this room yet, but with your permission **yo** shall do so now."

As he spoke, he whipped a tape measure and a large round magnifying glass **de su bolsillo**. With these two implements he trotted noiselessly about the room, sometimes stopping, occasionally kneeling, and once lying flat upon **su** face. So engrossed **era** he with **su** occupation that he appeared to have forgotten our presence, for he chattered away **para** himself under **su** breath the whole time, keeping up a running fire **de** exclamations, groans, whistles, and little cries suggestive **de** encouragement and **de** hope. As **yo** watched him **era** irresistibly reminded **de un** pure - blooded well - trained foxhound as **eso** dashes backwards and forwards through the covert, whining **en** its eagerness, until **eso** comes across the lost scent. For twenty minutes or more he continued **sus** researches, measuring with the most exact care the distance between marks which were entirely invisible **para** me, and occasionally applying **su** tape **hacia** the walls **en** an equally incomprehensible manner. **En** one place he gathered up very carefully a little pile **de** grey dust **de** the floor, and packed it away **en** an envelope. Finally, he examined with **su** glass the word upon the wall, going over every letter **de eso** with the most minute exactness. This done, he appeared to be satisfied, for he replaced **su** tape and **su** glass **en su bolsillo**.

"They say that genius is an infinite capacity for taking pains," he remarked with a smile. "**Eso** is a very bad definition, but **eso** does apply to detective work."

Gregson and Lestrade had watched the manoeuvres of their amateur companion with considerable curiosity and some contempt. They evidently failed to appreciate the fact, which **yo** had begun to realize, that Sherlock Holmes' smallest actions were all directed towards some definite and practical end.

"What do **tú** think **de eso**, sir?" they both asked.

"It would be robbing you **de** the credit **de** the case if I was to presume to **ayudar** you," remarked my friend. "**Tú** are doing so well now that **eso** would be a pity for anyone to interfere." There **era un mundo de** sarcasm **en su** voice as he spoke. "If **tú** will let me know how your investigations go," he continued, "**yo** shall be happy to give you any **ayuda** **yo** can. **En** the meantime **yo** should like to speak **a** the constable who found the body. Can **tú** give me **su** name and address?"

Lestrade glanced at **su** note - book. "John Rance," he said. "He is off duty now. **Tú** will find him at 46, Audley Court, Kennington Park Gate."

Holmes took a note **de** the address.

"Come along, Doctor," he said; "we shall **ir** and look him up. **Yo** will tell you one thing, which may **ayudar** you **en** the case," he continued, turning **a los** two detectives. "There has been murder done, and the murderer **era** a man. He **era** more than six **pies** high, was **en** the prime **de vida**, had small **pies** for **su** height, wore coarse, square - toed boots and smoked a Trichinopoly cigar. He came here with **su** victim **en** a four - wheeled cab, which **era** drawn by a horse with three old shoes and one new one on **su** off fore leg. **En** all probability the murderer had a florid face, and the finger - nails **de su** right hand were remarkably long. These are only **unas pocas** indications, but they may assist you."

Lestrade and Gregson glanced at <u>**cada**</u> other with an incredulous smile.

"If this man **era** murdered, how **era eso** done?" asked the former.

"Poison," said Sherlock Holmes curtly, and strode off. "One other thing, Lestrade," he added, turning round at the door: "'Rache,' is the German for 'revenge;' so don't lose your time looking for Miss Rachel."

With which Parthian shot he walked away, leaving the two rivals open - mouthed behind him.

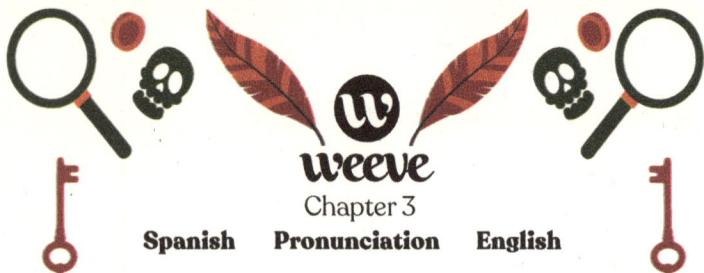

Spanish	Pronunciation	English
yo	io	i
su	su	his
sin embargo	sin embargo	however
you	iou	you
podrías	podɾjas	you might
que	ke	that
ayudar	aiudaɾ	help
mejor	mexoɾ	best
por supuesto	poɾ supwesto	of course
palabras	palabɾas	words
ayuda	aiuda	help
cada	kada	each

4

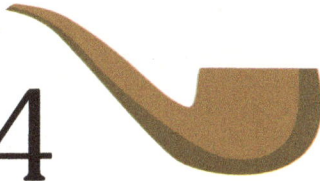

WHAT JOHN RANCE HAD TO TELL

It was one of the clock when we left No. 3, Lauriston Gardens. Sherlock Holmes led me **a la** nearest telegraph office, whence he dispatched a long telegram. He then hailed a cab, and ordered the driver to take us **hacia** the address given us **por** Lestrade.

"There is nothing like first hand evidence," he remarked; "as a matter **de** fact, my mind is entirely made up upon the case, but still we may as well learn all **eso** is to be learned."

"**Tú** amaze me, Holmes," said **yo**. "Surely **tú no estás** as sure as **tú** pretend to be **de** all those particulars which **tú** gave."

"There has no room for a mistake," he answered. "The very **primera** thing which **yo** observed on arriving there **era** that a cab had made two ruts with its wheels close **a** the curb. Now, up to last night, we have had no rain for a week, so that those wheels which left such a deep impression must have been there during the night. There were the marks **de** the horse's hoofs, too, the outline **de uno de** which **era** far more clearly cut than that **del** other three, showing that **eso era** a new shoe. Since the cab **era** there after the rain began, and **no estaba** there at **ninguna** time during the morning -- **yo** have Gregson's word for that -- it follows that **eso** must have been there during the night, and, therefore, that **eso** brought those two individuals **hacia** the house."

31

"**Eso** seems simple enough," said **yo**; "but how <u>**sobre**</u> the other man's height?"

"Why, the height **de** a man, **en** nine cases out **de** ten, can be told **de** the length **de su** stride. **Eso** is a simple calculation enough, though there is no use my boring you with figures. **Yo** had this fellow's stride both on the clay outside and on the dust within. Then **yo** had a way **de** checking my calculation. When a man writes on a wall, **su** instinct leads him to write **sobre** the level **de sus** own eyes. Now that writing **era** just over six **pies de** the ground. **Era** child's play."

"And **su** age?" **Yo** asked.

"Well, <u>**si**</u> a man can stride four and a - half **pies** without the smallest effort, he can't be quite **en** the sere and yellow. **Eso fue** the breadth **de** a puddle on the garden walk which he had evidently walked across. Patent - leather boots had gone round, and Square - toes had hopped over. There is no **misterio sobre eso** at all. **Yo** am simply applying to ordinary **vida unos pocos de** those precepts **de** observation and deduction which **yo** advocated **en** that article. Is there anything else **que** puzzles you?"

"The finger nails and the Trichinopoly," **yo** suggested.

"The writing on the wall **era** done with a man's forefinger dipped **en** blood. My glass allowed me to observe that the plaster **era** slightly scratched **en** doing **eso**, which would not have been the case **si** the man's nail had been trimmed. **Yo** gathered up some scattered ash **de** the floor. **Era** dark **en** colour and flakey -- such an ash as is only made **por un** Trichinopoly. **Yo** have made a special study **de** cigar ashes -- **en** fact, **yo** have written a monograph upon the subject. **Yo** flatter myself that **yo** can distinguish at a glance the ash **de cualquier** known brand, either **de** cigar or **de** tobacco. It is just **en** such details that the skilled detective differs from the Gregson and Lestrade type."

"And the florid face?" **Yo** asked.

"Ah, **eso era** a more daring shot, though **yo** have no doubt that **yo estaba** right. **Tú** must not ask me that at the present state **de** the affair."

Yo passed my hand over my brow. "My head is **en** a whirl," **yo** remarked; "the more **uno** thinks **de eso** the more mysterious **eso** grows. How came these two men -- **si** there were two men -- into an empty house? What has become **de** the cabman who drove them? How could **un** man compel **otro** to take poison? Where did the blood come from? What **era** the object **de** the murderer, since robbery had no part **en** it? How came the woman's ring there? Above all, why should the second man write up the German word Rache **antes de** decamping? **Yo** confess that **yo**

32

can not see **alguna** possible way **de** reconciling all these facts."

My companion smiled approvingly.

"**Tú** sum up the difficulties **de** the situation succinctly and well," he said. "There is much **que** is still obscure, though **yo** have quite made up my mind on the main facts. As to poor Lestrade's discovery **era** simply a blind intended to put the police upon a wrong track, by suggesting Socialism and secret societies. **Eso** was not done **por un** German. The A, **si tú** noticed, was printed somewhat after the German fashion. Now, a real German invariably prints **en** the Latin character, so that we may safely say that this **era** not written **por uno**, but **por un** clumsy imitator who overdid **su** part. **Era** simply a ruse to divert inquiry into a wrong channel. **Yo** am not going to tell you much more **de** the case, Doctor. **Tú** know a conjuror gets no credit when once he has explained **su** trick, and **si yo** show you too much **de** my method **de** working, **tú** will come **a** the conclusion that **yo** am a very ordinary individual after all."

"**Yo** shall never **hacer** that," **yo** answered; "**tú** have brought detection as near an exact science as **eso** ever will be brought **en** this **mundo**."

My companion flushed up with pleasure at my **palabras**, and the earnest way **en** which **yo** uttered them. **Yo** had already observed that he **era** as sensitive to flattery on the score **de su** art as any girl could be **de ella** beauty.

"**Yo** will tell you one other thing," he said. "Patent leathers and Square - toes came **en** the same cab, and they walked down the pathway together as friendly as possible -- arm - **en** - arm, **en** all probability. When they got inside they walked up and down the room -- or rather, Patent - leathers stood still while Square - toes walked up and down. **Yo** could read all that **en** the dust; and **yo** could read that as he walked he grew more and more excited. That is shown **por el** increased length **de su** strides. He was talking all the while, and working himself up, no doubt, into a fury. Then the tragedy occurred. **Yo** have told you all **yo** know myself now, for the rest is mere surmise and conjecture. We have a good working basis, **sin embargo**, on which to start. We must hurry up, for **yo** want to **ir a** Halle's concert to hear Norman Neruda this afternoon."

This conversation had occurred while our cab had been threading its way through a long succession **de** dingy streets and dreary by - ways. **En** the dingiest and dreariest of them our driver suddenly came **a** a stand. "**Eso** **tiene** Audley Court **en** there," he said, pointing **a un** narrow slit **en** the line **de** dead - coloured brick. "**Tú** will find me here when **tú** come back."

Audley Court **no era** an attractive locality. The narrow passage led us into a quadrangle paved with flags and lined **por** sordid dwellings. We picked our way among groups **de** dirty children, and through lines **de** discoloured linen, until we came **a** Number 46, the door **de** which **estaba** decorated with a small slip **de** brass on which the name Rance **era** engraved. On enquiry we found that the constable **estaba en** bed, and we were shown into a little front parlour to await **su** coming.

He appeared presently, looking a little irritable at being disturbed **en sus** slumbers. "**Yo** made my report at the office," he said.

Holmes took a half - sovereign **de su bolsillo** and played with it pensively. "We thought that we should like to hear it all **de** your own lips," he said.

"**Yo** shall be most happy to tell you anything **yo** can," the constable answered with **sus** eyes upon the little golden disk.

"Just let us hear **eso** all **en** your own way as **eso** occurred."

Rance sat down on the horsehair sofa, and knitted **sus** brows as though determined not to omit anything **en su** narrative.

"**Yo** will tell **eso** ye **de** the beginning," he said. "My time is **de** ten at night **a** six **en** the morning. At eleven **había** a fight at the 'WhiteHart'; but bar **eso** all **era** quiet enough on the beat. At **una de** the clock it began to rain, and **yo** met Harry Murcher -- him who **tiene** the Holland Grove beat -- and we stood together at the corner **de** Henrietta Street **a** - talkin'. Presently -- maybe **sobre** two or a little after -- **yo** thought **yo** would take a look round and see that all **era** right down the Brixton Road. **Era** precious dirty and lonely. Not a soul did **yo** meet all the way down, though a cab or two went past me. **Era** a strollin' down, thinkin' between ourselves how uncommon handy a four **de** gin hot would be, when suddenly the glint **de** a light caught my eye **en** the window **de esa** same house. Now, **yo** knew that them two houses **en** Lauriston Gardens **era** empty on account **de él que** owns them who won't have the drains seen to, though the very last tenant what lived **en uno de ellos** diedo' typhoid fever. **Era** knocked all **en** a heap therefore at seeing a light **en** the window, and **yo** suspected as something **estaba** wrong. When **yo** got **a** the door----"

"**Tú** stopped, and then walked back **a** the garden gate," my companion interrupted. "What did **tú haces** that for?"

Rance gave a violent jump, and stared at Sherlock Holmes with the utmost amazement upon **sus** features.

"Why, **eso** is true, sir," he said; "though how **tú** come to know **eso**, Heaven only knows. Ye see, when **yo** got up **a** the door **era** so still and so lonesome, that **yo** thought **yo** would be none the worse for some one with me. **Yo** ain't afeared **de** anything on this sideo' the grave; but **yo** thought that maybe **era** him that diedo' the typhoid inspecting the drains what killed him. The thought gave me a kindo' turn, and **yo** walked back **hacia** the gate to see **si yo** could see Murcher's lantern, but **no había** no sign **de él** nor **de** anyone else."

"There was **<u>nadie</u> en** the street?"

"Not a livin' soul, sir, nor as much as a dog. Then **yo** pulled myself together and went back and pushed the door open. All **estaba** quiet inside, so **yo** went into the room where the light **era** a - burnin'. **Había** a candle flickerin' on the mantelpiece -- a red wax one -- and **por** its light **yo** saw----"

"Yes, **yo** know all that **tú** saw. **Tú** walked round the room several times, and **tú** knelt down **por** the body, and then **tú** walked through and tried the kitchen door, and then----"

John Rance sprang **para sus pies** with a frightened face and suspicion **en sus** eyes. "Where was **tú** hid to see all that?" he cried. "**Eso** seems **para** me that **tú** knows a deal more than **tú** should."

Holmes laughed and threw **su** card across the table **hacia** the constable. "Don't get arresting me for the murder," he said. "**Yo** am **uno de** the hounds and not the wolf; Mr. Gregson or Mr. Lestrade will answer for that. Go on, though. What did **tú haces** next?"

Rance resumed **su** seat, without **sin embargo** losing **su** mystified expression. "**Yo** went back **hacia** the gate and sounded my whistle. **Eso** brought Murcher and two more **a** the spot."

"Was the street empty then?"

"Well, **estaba**, as far as anybody that could be **de cualquier** good goes."

"What do **tú** mean?"

The constable's features broadened into a grin. "**Yo** have seen many a drunk chap **en** my time," he said, "but never anyone so cryin' drunk as that cove. He **estaba** at the gate when **yo** came out, a - leanin' up agin the railings, and a - singin' at the pitcho' **sus** lungs **sobre** Columbine's New - fangled Banner, or some such stuff. He couldn't stand, far less **ayudar**."

"What sort **de** a man **era** he?" asked Sherlock Holmes.

John Rance appeared to be somewhat irritated at this digression. "He **era** an uncommon drunk sorto' man," he said. "He had ha' found hisself **en** the station **si** we hadn't been so took up."

"**Su** face -- **su** dress -- did not **tú** notice them?" Holmes broke **en** impatiently.

"**Yo** should think **yo** did notice them, seeing that **yo** had to prop him up -- me and Murcher between us. He **era** a long chap, with a red face, the lower part muffled round----"

"**Eso** will do," cried Holmes. "What became **de él**?"

"We would enough to **hacer** without lookin' after him," the policeman said, **en** an aggrieved voice. "**Yo** will wager he found **su** way home all right."

"How **estaba** he dressed?"

"A brown overcoat."

"Had he a whip **en su** hand?"

"A whip -- no."

"He must have left **eso** behind," muttered my companion. "**Tú** did not happen to see or hear a cab after that?"

"No."

"There is a half - sovereign for you," my companion said, standing up and taking **su** hat. "**Yo** am afraid, Rance, that **tú** will never rise **en** the force. That head **de** yours should be for use as well as ornament. **Podrías** have gained your sergeant's stripes last night. The man whom **usted** held **en** your hands is the man who holds the clue **de** this **misterio**, and whom we are seeking. There is no use **de** arguing **sobre eso** now; **yo** tell you that **eso** is so. Come along, Doctor."

We started off for the cab together, leaving our informant incredulous, but obviously uncomfortable.

"The blundering fool," Holmes said, bitterly, as we drove back **hacia** our lodgings. "Just to think **de** his having such an incomparable bit **de** good luck, and not taking advantage **de eso**."

"**Yo** am rather **en** the dark still. **Eso** is true that the description **de** this man tallies with your idea **del** second party **en** this **misterio**. But why should he come back **a** the house after leaving **eso**? **Eso** is not the way **de** criminals."

"The ring, man, the ring: **eso fue** what he came back for. **Si** we have no other way **de** catching him, we can always bait our line with the ring. **Yo** shall have him, Doctor -- **yo** will lay you two to **uno** that **yo** have him. **Yo** must thank you for **eso** all. **Puede que yo no** have gone but for you, and so have missed the finest study **yo** ever came across: a study **en** scarlet, eh? Why shouldn't we use a little art jargon. There is the scarlet thread **de** murder running through the colourless skein **de vida**, and our duty is to unravel **eso**, and isolate **eso**, and expose every inch **de eso**. And now for lunch, and then for Norman Neruda. Her attack and her bowing **están** splendid. What is that little thing **de** Chopin's she plays so magnificently: Tra - la - la - lira - lira - lay."

Leaning back **en** the cab, this amateur bloodhound carolled away like a lark while **yo** meditated upon the many - sidedness **del** human mind.

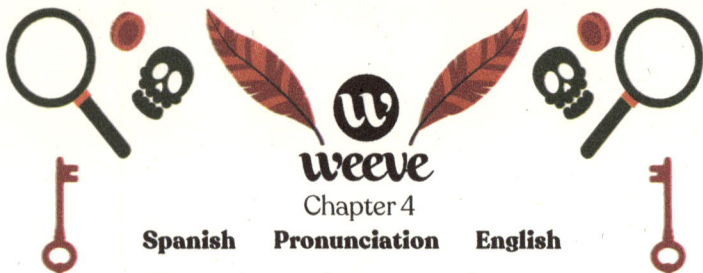

Spanish	Pronunciation	English
ninguna	ningwna	any
sobre	sobre	about
si	si	if
alguna	algwna	any
hacer	aser	do
tiene	tjene	has
nadie	nadje	no one
usted	usted	you
están	estan	are

5

OUR ADVERTISEMENT BRINGS A VISITOR

Weeve Reading Tip: Translating words will make it more difficult to enter a flow state. This is where the natural process of language learning is most powerful. In this state your brain has the strongest ability to learn a language

Our morning's exertions had been too much for my weak health, and **era** tired out **en** the afternoon. After Holmes' departure for the concert, **yo** lay down upon the sofa and endeavoured to get a couple **de** hours' sleep. **Era** a useless attempt. My mind had been too much excited **por** all that had occurred, and the strangest fancies and surmises crowded into **eso**. Every time that **yo** closed my eyes **yo** saw **antes de** me the distorted baboon - like countenance **del** murdered man. <u>**Tan**</u> sinister **era** the impression which that face had produced upon me that **yo** found **eso** difficult to feel anything but gratitude for him who had removed its owner **del mundo**. **Si** ever human features bespoke vice **del** most malignant type, they were certainly those **de** Enoch J. Drebber, **de** Cleveland. Still **yo** recognized that justice must be done, and that the depravity **de** the victim **era** no condonment **en** the eyes **de** the law.

The more **yo** thought **de eso** the more extraordinary did my companion's hypothesis, that the man had been poisoned, appear. **Yo** remembered how he had sniffed **sus** lips, and had no doubt that he had detected something which had given rise **a** the idea. <u>**Entonces**</u>, again, **si** not poison, what had caused the man's death, since there was neither wound nor marks **de** strangulation? But, on the **otra** hand, whose blood **era esa** which lay **tan** thickly upon the floor? There were no signs **de** a struggle, nor had the victim **alguna** weapon with which he <u>**podría**</u> have wounded an

39

antagonist. As long as all these questions were unsolved, **yo** felt that sleep would be no easy matter, either for Holmes **o** myself. **Su** quiet self - confident manner convinced me that he had already formed a theory which explained all the facts, though what **era yo** could not for an **instante** conjecture.

He **era** very late **en** returning -- **tan** late, that **yo** knew that the concert could not have detained him all the time. Dinner **era** on the table **antes de** he appeared.

"**Fue** magnificent," he said, as he took **su** seat. "Do **tú** remember what Darwin says **sobre** music? He claims that the power **de** producing and appreciating it existed among the human race long **antes de** the power **de** speech was arrived at. Perhaps **eso** is why we **estamos tan** subtly influenced **por eso**. **Hay** vague memories **en** our souls **de** those misty centuries when **el mundo era en** its childhood."

"**Eso** is rather a broad idea," **yo** remarked.

"One's ideas must be as broad as Nature **si** they **están** to interpret Nature," he answered. "What is the matter? You are not looking quite yourself. This Brixton Road affair has upset you."

"To tell the truth, it has," **yo** said. "**Yo** ought to be more case - hardened after my Afghan experiences. **Yo** saw my own comrades hacked to pieces at Maiwand without losing my nerve."

"**Yo** can understand. There is **un misterio sobre** this which stimulates the imagination; where there is no imagination there is no horror. Have **tú** seen the evening paper?"

"No."

"**Eso** gives a fairly good account **de** the affair. **Eso** does not mention the fact that when the man **era** raised up, a woman's wedding ring fell upon the floor. **Eso** is just as well it does not."

"Why?"

"**Mira** at this advertisement," he answered. "**Yo** had **uno** sent **a** every paper this morning immediately after the affair."

He threw the paper across **para** me and **yo** glanced at the place indicated. **Era** the **primer** announcement **en** the "Found" column. "**En** Brixton Road, this morning," it ran, "a plain gold wedding ring, found **en** the roadway between the 'WhiteHart' Tavern and Holland Grove. Apply Dr. Watson, 221B, Baker Street, between eight and nine this evening."

"Excuse my using your name," he said. "**Si yo** used my own some **de** these dunderheads would recognize it, and want to meddle **en** the affair."

"**Eso** is all right," **yo** answered. "But supposing anyone applies, **yo** have no ring."

"Oh yes, **tú** have," said he, handing me **uno**. "This will **hacer** very well. **Eso** is almost a facsimile."

"And who do **tú** expect will answer this advertisement."

"Why, the man **en** the brown coat -- our florid friend with the square toes. **Si** he does not come himself he will send an accomplice."

"Would he not consider **eso** as too dangerous?"

"Not at all. **Si** my view **de** the case is correct, and **yo** have every reason to believe that **eso** is, this man would rather risk anything than lose the ring. According **para** my notion he dropped **eso** while stooping **sobre** Drebber's body, and did not miss **eso** at the time. After leaving the house he discovered **su** loss and hurried back, but found the police already **en** possession, owing **para su** own folly **en** leaving the candle burning. He had to pretend to be drunk **en** order to allay the suspicions which **podría** have been aroused **por su** appearance at the gate. Now put yourself **en** that man's place. On thinking the matter over, **eso** must have occurred **para** him that **era** possible that he had lost the ring **en** the road after leaving the house. What would he **hacer, entonces**? He would eagerly look out for the evening papers **en** the hope **de** seeing **eso** among the articles found. **Su** eye, **por supuesto**, would light upon this. He would be overjoyed. Why **debería** he fear a trap? There would be no reason **en sus** eyes why the finding **de** the ring **debería** be connected.with the murder. He would come. He will come. **Tú** shall see him within an hour?"

"And **entonces**?" **Yo** asked.

"Oh, **tú** can leave me to deal with him **entonces**. Have **tú alguna** arms?"

"**Yo** have my old service revolver and **unos pocos** cartridges."

"**Tú** had better clean **eso** and load **eso**. He will be a desperate man, and though **yo** shall take him unawares, it is as well to be ready for anything."

Yo went **a** my bedroom and followed **su** advice. When **yo** returned with the pistol the table had been cleared, and Holmes **era** engaged **en su** favourite occupation **de** scraping upon **su** violin.

"The plot thickens," he said, as **yo** entered; "**yo** have just had an answer **para** my American telegram. My view **de** the case is the correct one."

"And **ese** is?" **Yo** asked eagerly.

"My fiddle would be the better for new strings," he remarked. "Put your pistol **en** your **bolsillo**. When **el compañero** comes speak **para** him **en** an ordinary way. Leave the rest **para** me. Don't frighten him **por** looking at him too hard."

"It is eight **de** the clock now," **yo** said, glancing at my watch.

"Yes. He will probably be here **en unos pocos** minutes. Open the door slightly. **Eso** will do. Now put the key on the inside. **Gracias**! This is a queer old book **yo** picked up at a stall yesterday-- 'DeJure inter Gentes'--published **en** Latin at Liege **en** the Lowlands, **en** 1642. Charles' head **era** still firm on **sus** shoulders when this little brown - backed volume **era** struck off."

"Who is the printer?"

"Philippe de Croy, whoever he may have been. On the fly - leaf, **en** very faded ink, is written 'Exlibris Guliolmi Whyte.' **Yo** wonder who William Whyte **era**. Some pragmatical seventeenth century lawyer, **yo** suppose. **Su** writing **tiene** a legal twist **sobre eso**. Here comes our man, **creo**."

As he spoke there was a sharp ring at the bell. Sherlock Holmes rose softly and moved **su** chair **en** the direction **de** the door. We heard the servant pass along the hall, and the sharp click **de** the latch as she opened it.

"Does Dr. Watson live here?" asked a clear but rather harsh voice. We could not hear the servant's reply, but the door closed, and **alguien** began to ascend the stairs. The footfall **era** an uncertain and shuffling one. **Una mirada de** surprise passed **sobre** the face **de** my companion as he listened **para eso**. **Eso** came slowly along the passage, and there was a feeble tap at the door.

"Come in," **yo** cried.

At my summons, instead **de** the man **de** violence whom we expected, a very old and wrinkled woman hobbled into the apartment. She appeared to be dazzled **por el** sudden blaze **de** light, and after dropping a curtsey, she stood blinking at us with her bleared eyes and fumbling **en** her **bolsillo** with nervous, shaky fingers. **Yo** glanced at my companion, and **su** face had assumed such a disconsolate expression that **era** all **yo** could **hacer** to keep my countenance.

The old crone drew **fuera** an evening paper, and pointed at our advertisement. "**Eso** is this as has brought me, good gentlemen," she said, dropping **otro** curtsey; "a gold wedding ring **en** the Brixton Road. **Eso** belongs **para** my girl Sally, as **era** married only this time twelvemonth, which her husband is steward aboard a Union boat, and what he would say **si** he come 'omeand found her without her ring is more than **yo** can **pensar**, he being short enough at the **mejor**o' times, but more especially when he

tiene the drink. **Si eso** please you, she went **a** the circus last night along with----"

"Is **ese** her ring?" **Yo** asked.

"The Lord be thanked!" cried the old woman; "Sally will be a glad woman this night. **Ese** is the ring."

"And what may your address be?" **Yo** inquired, taking up a pencil.

"13, Duncan Street, Houndsditch. A weary way **de** here."

"The Brixton Road does not lie between **ningún** circus and Houndsditch," said Sherlock Holmes sharply.

The old woman faced round and looked keenly at him **de** her little red - rimmed eyes. "**El caballero** asked me for my address," she said. "Sally lives **en** lodgings at 3, Mayfield Place, Peckham."

"And your name is----?"

"My name is Sawyer -- her's is Dennis, which Tom Dennis married her -- and a smart, clean lad, too, as long as he is at sea, and no steward **en** the company more thought **de**; but when on shore, what with the women and what with liquor shops----"

"Here is your ring, Mrs. Sawyer," **yo** interrupted, **en** obedience **a** a sign **de** my companion; "**eso** clearly belongs **a** your daughter, and **yo** am glad to be able to restore **eso al** rightful owner."

With many mumbled blessings and protestations **de** gratitude the old crone packed **eso** away **en** her **bolsillo**, and shuffled off down the stairs. Sherlock Holmes sprang **para sus pies** the moment that she **era** gone and rushed into **su** room. He returned **en unos pocos** seconds enveloped **en** an ulster and a cravat. "**Yo** will follow her," he said, hurriedly; "she must be an accomplice, and will lead me **hacia** him. Wait up for me." The hall door had hardly slammed behind our visitor **antes de** Holmes had descended the stair. Looking through the window **yo** could see her walking feebly along the **otro** side, while her pursuer dogged her some little distance behind. "Either **su** whole theory is incorrect," **yo** thought **para** myself, "o else he will be led now **a** the heart **del misterio**." There was no need for him to ask me to wait up for him, for **yo** felt that sleep **era** impossible until **yo** heard the result **de su** adventure.

Era close upon nine when he set **fuera**. **Yo** had no idea how long he **puedía estar**, but **yo** sat stolidly puffing at my pipe and skipping **sobre** the pages **de** Henri Murger's "Vie dc Bohème." Ten **de** the clock passed, and **yo** heard the footsteps **de** the maid as they pattered off **hacia** bed. Eleven, and the more stately tread **de** the landlady passed my door, bound for the same destination.

Era close upon twelve **antes de yo** heard the sharp sound **de su** latch - key. **El instante** he entered **yo** saw **por su** face that he had not been successful. Amusement and chagrin seemed to be struggling for the mastery, until the former suddenly carried the day, and he burst into a hearty laugh.

"**Yo** wouldn't have the Scotland Yarders know **eso** for **el mundo**," he cried, dropping into **su** chair; "**yo** have chaffed them **tanto** that they would never have let me hear the end **de eso**. **Yo** can afford to laugh, **porque yo** know that **yo** will be **incluso** with **ellos en** the long run."

"What is **eso entonces**?" **Yo** asked.

"Oh, **yo** don't mind telling a story against myself. That creature had gone a little way when she began to limp and show every sign **de** being foot - sore. Presently she came to a halt, and hailed a four - wheeler which was passing. **Yo** managed to be close **a** her **tanto** as to hear the address, but **yo** need not have been **tan** anxious, for she sang it out loud enough to be heard at the **otro** side **de** the street, 'Drive**hacia** 13, Duncan Street, Houndsditch,' she cried. This begins to **parecer** genuine, **yo** thought, and having seen her safely inside, **yo** perched myself behind. **Ese** is an art which every detective **debería** be an expert at. Well, away we rattled, and never drew rein until we reached the street **en** question. **Yo** hopped off **antes de que** we came to the door, and strolled down the street **en** an easy, lounging way. **Yo** saw the cab pull up. The driver jumped down, and **yo** saw him open the door and stand expectantly. Nothing came **fuera** though. When **yo** reached him he was groping about frantically **en** the empty cab, and giving vent **al** finest assorted collection **de** oaths that ever **yo** listened to. **No había** sign o trace **de su** passenger, and **yo** fear **eso** will be some time **antes de que** he gets **su** fare. On inquiring at Number 13 we found that the house belonged **a un** respectable paperhanger, named Keswick, and that **nadie de** the name either **de** Sawyer o Dennis had ever been heard **de** there."

"**Tú** don't mean to say," **yo** cried, **en** amazement, "that that tottering, feeble old woman **era** able to get **fuera de** the cab while **era en** motion, without either **tú** o the driver seeing her?"

"Old woman be damned!" said Sherlock Holmes, sharply. "We were the old women to be **tan** taken in. **Eso** must have been a young man, and an **uno activo**, too, besides being an incomparable actor. The get - up **era** inimitable. He saw that he **era** followed, no doubt, and used this means **de** giving me the slip. **Eso** shows that the man we **estamos** after is not as lonely as **yo** imagined he **era**, but **tiene** friends who **están** ready to risk something for him. Now, Doctor, **tú** are looking done - up. Take my advice and turn in."

Yo estaba certainly feeling very weary, **asi que yo** obeyed **su**

injunction. **Yo** left Holmes seated **en** front **del** smouldering fire, and long into the watches **de** the night **yo** heard the low, melancholy wailings **de su** violin, and knew that he was still pondering **sobre** the strange problem which he had set himself to unravel.

Spanish	Pronunciation	English
tan	tan	so
entonces	entonses	then
podría	podrja	might
o	o	or
estamos	estamos	are
hay	ai	there are
mira	mira	look
debería	deberja	should
gracias	grasias	thank you
creo	kreo	i think
alguien	algien	some one
fuera	fwera	out
pensar	pensar	think
ningún	ningwn	any
puedía estar	pwedja estar	might be
tanto	tanto	so much
parecer	pareser	look

6

TOBIAS GREGSON SHOWS WHAT HE CAN DO

The papers next day were full **del** "Brixton **Misterio**," as they termed it. Each had a long account **de** the affair, and some had leaders upon **eso en** addition. **Había** some information **en ellos** which **era** new **para** me. **Yo** still retain **en** my scrap - book numerous clippings and extracts bearing upon the case. Here is a condensation **de unos pocos de ellos**: --

The Daily Telegraph remarked that **en** the history **d e l crimen** there had seldom been a tragedy which presented stranger features. The German name **de** the victim, the absence **de todo otro** motive, and the sinister inscription on the wall, **todo** pointed **hacia** its perpetration **por** political refugees and revolutionists. The Socialists had many branches **en** America, and the deceased had, no doubt, infringed **su** unwritten laws, and been tracked down **por ellos**. After alluding airily **al** Vehmgericht, aqua tofana, Carbonari, the Marchioness de Brinvilliers, the Darwinian theory, the principles **de** Malthus, and the Ratcliff Highway murders, the article concluded **por** admonishing the Government and advocating a closer watch **sobre** foreigners **en** England.

The Standard commented upon the fact that lawless outrages **de** the sort usually occurred under a Liberal Administration. They arose **desde el** unsettling **de** the minds **de** the masses, and the consequent weakening **de toda** authority. The deceased **era** an

American **caballero** who had been residing for some weeks **en** the Metropolis. He had stayed at the boarding - house **de** Madame Charpentier, **en** Torquay Terrace, Camberwell. He **era** accompanied **en sus** travels **por su** private secretary, Mr. Joseph Stangerson. The two bade adieu to **su** landlady upon Tuesday, the 4th inst., and departed **para** Euston Station with the avowed intention **de** catching the Liverpool express. They were afterwards seen together upon the platform. Nothing more is known **de ellos** until **el señor** Drebber's body **fue**, as recorded, discovered **en** an empty house **en** the Brixton Road, many miles **de** Euston. How he came there, **o** how he met **su** fate, are questions which **están** still involved **en misterio**. Nothing is known **de** the whereabouts **de** Stangerson. We **estamos** glad to learn that **el señor** Lestrade and **el señor** Gregson, **de** Scotland Yard, are both engaged upon the case, and **eso** is confidently anticipated that these well - known officers will speedily throw light upon the matter.

The Daily News observed that **había** no doubt as to **el crimen** being **uno político**. The despotism and hatred **de** Liberalism which animated the Continental Governments had had the effect **de** driving **hacia** our shores a number **de** men who <u>**podrían**</u> have made excellent citizens were they not soured **por** the recollection **de todo** that they had undergone. Among these men **había** a stringent code **de** honour, **cualquier** infringement **de** which **era** punished **por** death. Every effort <u>**deberían**</u> be made to <u>**encontrar**</u> the secretary, Stangerson, and to ascertain some particulars **de** the habits **del** deceased. A great step had been gained **por** the discovery **de** the address **de** the house at which he had boarded -- a result which **era** entirely due **a** the acuteness and energy **de el señor** Gregson **de** Scotland Yard.

Sherlock Holmes and **yo** read these notices over together at breakfast, and they appeared to afford him considerable amusement.

"**Yo** told **a ti** that, whatever happened, Lestrade and Gregson would be sure to score."

"**Eso** depends on how **eso** turns out."

"Oh, bless **a ti**, **eso** doesn't matter **en** the least. **Si** the man is caught, **eso** will be on account **de sus** exertions; **si** he escapes, **eso** will be **en** spite **de sus** exertions. It is heads **yo** win and tails **tú** lose. Whatever they **hacer**, they will <u>**tener**</u> followers. 'Unsot trouve toujours un plus sot qui l'admire.'"

"What on earth is this?" **Yo** cried, for at this moment there came the pattering **de** many **pasos en** the hall and on the stairs, accompanied **por** audible expressions **de** disgust upon the part **de** our landlady.

"**Eso** is the Baker Street division of the detective police force," said my **compañero**, gravely; and as he spoke there rushed into the room half a dozen **de** the dirtiest and most ragged street Arabs that ever **yo** clapped eyes on.

"'Tention!" cried Holmes, **en** a sharp tone, and the six dirty little scoundrels stood **en** a line like **tantos** many disreputable statuettes. "**En** future **tú** shall send up Wiggins alone to report, and the rest **de ti** must wait **en** the street. Have you found **eso**, Wiggins?"

"No, sir, we hain't," said **uno de** the youths.

"**Yo** hardly expected **tú** would. **Tú** must keep on until **tú haces**. Here **están** your wages." He handed **cada de ellos** a shilling.

"Now, off **vete**, and come back with a better report next time."

He waved **su** hand, and they scampered away downstairs like **tantas** many rats, and we heard **sus** shrill voices next moment **en** the street.

"There is more work to be got **fuera de uno de** those little beggars than **fuera de** a dozen **de** the force," Holmes remarked. "The mere sight **de un** official - looking person seals men's **labios**. These youngsters, **sin embargo**, **van** everywhere and hear everything. They **están** as sharp as needles, too; **todo** they want is organisation."

"Is it on this Brixton case that **tú** are employing **a ellos**?" **Yo** asked.

"Yes; there is a point which **yo** wish to ascertain. **Eso** is merely a matter **de** time. Hullo! we are going to hear some news now with a vengeance! Here is Gregson coming down the road with beatitude written upon every feature **de su** face. Bound for us, **yo** know. Yes, he is stopping. There he is!"

There was a violent peal at the bell, and **en unos pocos** seconds the fair - haired **detective** came up the stairs, three **pasos** at a time, and burst into our sitting - room.

"My dear **compañero**," he cried, wringing Holmes' unresponsive hand, "congratulate me! **Yo** have made the whole thing as clear as day."

A shade **de** anxiety seemed **para** me to cross my companion's expressive face.

"Do **tú** mean that **tú estás** on the right track?" he asked.

"The right track! Why, sir, we **tenemos** the man under lock and key."

"And **su** name is?"

"Arthur Charpentier, sub - lieutenant **en** Her Majesty's navy," cried Gregson, pompously, rubbing **su** fat hands and inflating **su** chest.

Sherlock Holmes gave a sigh **de** relief, and relaxed into a smile.

"Take a seat, and try **uno de** these cigars," he said. "We **estamos** anxious to know how **tú** managed **eso**. Will you have some whiskey and water?"

"**Yo** don't mind **si** I do," **el detective** answered. "The tremendous exertions which **yo** have gone through during the last day **o** two have worn me out. Not so much bodily exertion, **tú** understand, as the strain upon the mind. **Tú** will appreciate that, **señor** Sherlock Holmes, for we <u>**somos**</u> both brain - workers."

"**Tú haces** me too much honour," said Holmes, gravely. "Let us hear how **tú** arrived at this most gratifying result."

El detective seated himself **en** the arm - chair, and puffed complacently at **su** cigar. **Entonces** suddenly he slapped **su** thigh **en** a paroxysm **de** amusement.

"The fun **de** it is," he cried, "that that fool Lestrade, who thinks himself **tan** smart, has gone off upon the wrong track altogether. He is after the secretary Stangerson, who had no more to **hacer** with **el crimen** than the babe unborn. **Yo tengo** no doubt that he has caught him by this time."

The idea tickled Gregson **tanto** that he laughed until he choked.

"And how did **tú** get your clue?"

"Ah, **yo** will tell **a ti todo sobre eso**. **Por supuesto**, Doctor Watson, this is strictly <u>**entre**</u> ourselves. The **primera** difficulty which we had to contend with **era** the finding **de** this American's antecedents. Some people would have waited until **su** advertisements were answered, **o** until parties came forward and volunteered information. **Esa** is not Tobias Gregson's way **de** going to work. **Tú** remember the hat beside the dead man?"

"Yes," said Holmes; "**por** John Underwood and Sons, 129, Camberwell Road."

Gregson looked quite crest - fallen.

"**Yo** had no idea that **tú** noticed that," he said. "Have **tú** been there?"

"No."

"Ha!" cried Gregson, **en** a relieved voice; "<u>**deberías**</u> never neglect a chance, **sin embargo** small it may seem."

"**Para una** great mind, nothing is little," remarked Holmes, sententiously.

"Well, **yo** went **a** Underwood, and asked him **si** he had sold a hat **de** that size and description. He looked **sobre sus** books, and came on it at once. He had sent the hat **a un señor** Drebber, residing at Charpentier's Boarding Establishment, Torquay Terrace. Thus **yo** got at **su** address."

"Smart -- very smart!" murmured Sherlock Holmes.

"**Yo** next called upon Madame Charpentier," continued **el detective**. "**Yo** found her very pale and distressed. Her daughter **estaba en** the room, too -- an uncommonly fine girl she is, too; she was looking red **sobre** the eyes and her **labios** trembled as **yo** spoke to her. **Eso** did not escape my notice. **Yo** began to smell a rat. **Tú** know the feeling, **señor** Sherlock Holmes, when **tú** come upon the right scent -- a kind **de** thrill **en** your nerves. 'Have **tú** heard **del** mysterious death **de** your late boarder **señor** Enoch J. Drebber, **de** Cleveland?' **Yo** asked.

"The mother nodded. She did not seem able to get **fuera** a word. The daughter burst into tears. **Yo** felt more than ever that these people knew something **de** the matter.

"'At what **de** the clock did **el señor** Drebber leave your house for the train?' **Yo** asked.

"'At eight **de** the clock,' she said, gulping **en** her throat to keep down her agitation. '**Su** secretary, **el señor** Stangerson, said that there were two trains -- **uno** at 9.15 and **uno** at 11. He was to catch the **primero**.

"'And **era eso** the last which **tú** saw **de él**?'

"A terrible change came **sobre** the woman's face as **yo** asked the question. Her features turned perfectly livid. **Era** some seconds **antes de que** she could get **fuera** the single word 'Yes'--and when **eso** did come **era en** a husky unnatural tone.

"**Hubo** silence for a moment, and **entonces** the daughter spoke **en** a calm clear voice.

"'No good can ever come **de** falsehood, mother,' she said. 'Let us be frank with this **caballero**. We did see **el señor** Drebber again.'

"'Qué **Dios** te perdone!' cried Madame Charpentier, throwing up her hands and sinking back **en** her chair. '**Tú** have murdered your brother.'

"'Arthur would rather that we spoke the truth,' the girl answered firmly.

"'**Tú** had **mejor** tell me **todo sobre eso** now,' **yo** said. 'Half-confidences **son** worse than none. Besides, **tú** do not know how much we know **de eso**.'

"'Onyour head be it, Alice!' cried her mother; and **entonces**, turning **para** me, 'yo will tell **a ti todo**, sir. Do not imagine that my agitation on behalf **de** my son arises **de cualquier** fear lest he **debería** have had a hand **en** this terrible affair. He is utterly innocent **de eso**. My dread is, **sin embargo**, that **en** your eyes and **en** the eyes **de** others he may appear to be compromised. **Eso sin embargo** is surely impossible. **Su** high character, **su** profession, **su** antecedents would **todos** forbid it.'

"'Yourmejor way is to make a clean breast **de** the facts,' yo answered. 'Dependupon **eso**, **si** your son is innocent he will be none the worse.'

"'Perhaps, Alice, **tú** had better leave us together,' she said, and her daughter withdrew. 'Now, sir,' she continued, 'yo had no intention **de** telling **a ti todo** this, **pero** since my poor daughter has disclosed **eso yo tengo** no alternative. Having once decided to speak, **yo** will tell **a ti todo** without omitting any particular.'

"'**Eso** is your wisest course,' said **yo**.

"'**El señor** Drebber has been with us nearly three weeks. He and **su** secretary, **el señor** Stangerson, had been travelling on the Continent. **Yo** noticed a "Copenhagen" label upon **cada uno de sus** trunks, showing that **ese** had been **su** last stopping place. Stangerson **era** a quiet reserved man, **pero su** employer, **yo** am sorry to say, was far otherwise. He **era** coarse **en sus** habits and brutish **en** his ways. The very night **de su** arrival he became very much the worse for drink, and, indeed, after twelve **de** the clock **en** the day he could hardly ever be said to be sober. **Sus** manners towards the maid - servants were disgustingly free and familiar. Worst **de todo**, he speedily assumed the same attitude towards my daughter, Alice, and spoke **a** her more than once **en** a way which, fortunately, she is too innocent to understand. On **una** occasion he actually seized her **en sus** arms and embraced her -- an outrage which caused **su** own secretary to reproach him for **su** unmanly conduct.'

"'**Pero** why did **tú** stand **todo** this,' **yo** asked. '**Yo** suppose that **tú** can get rid **de** your boarders when **tú** wish.'

"Mrs. Charpentier blushed at my pertinent question. 'Wouldto God that **yo** had given him notice on the very day that he came,' she said. '**Pero era** a sore temptation. They were paying a pound a day **cada uno** -- fourteen pounds a week, and this is the slack season. **Yo** am a widow, and my boy **en** the Navy has cost me much. **Yo** grudged to lose the money. **Yo** acted for the **mejor**. This last **era** too much, **sin embargo**, and **yo** gave him notice to leave on account **de eso**. **Esa era** the reason **de su** going.'

"'Well?'

"'Myheart grew light when **yo** saw him drive away. My son is on leave **justo** now, **pero yo** did not tell him anything **de todo** this, for **su** temper is violent, and he is passionately fond **de su** sister. When **yo** closed the door behind **de ellos** a load seemed to be lifted **de** my mind. Alas, **en** less than an hour **hubo** a ring at the bell, and **yo** learned that **el señor** Drebber had returned. He **era** much excited, and evidently the worse for drink. He forced **su** way into the room, where **yo** was sitting with my daughter, and made some incoherent remark **sobre** having missed **su** train. He **entonces** turned **para** Alice, and **antes de que** my very face, proposed **a** her that she **debería** fly with him. "You are **de** age," he said, "and there is no law to stop **a ti. Yo tengo** money enough and to spare. Never mind the old girl here, **pero** come along with me now straight away. **Tú** shall live like a princess." Poor Alice **estaba tan** frightened that she shrunk away **de** him, **pero** he caught her **por** the wrist and endeavoured to draw her towards the door. **Yo** screamed, and at that moment my son Arthur came into the room. What happened **entonces yo** do not know. **Yo** heard oaths and the confused sounds **de** a scuffle. **Yo estaba** too terrified to raise my head. When **yo** did **mirar** up **yo** saw Arthur standing **en** the doorway laughing, with a stick **en su** hand. "**No creo que** that fine **compañero** will trouble us again," he said. "**Yo** will **solo ir** after him and see what he does with himself." With those **palabras** he took **su** hat and started off down the street. The next morning we heard **de el señor** Drebber's mysterious death.'

"This statement came **de** Mrs. Charpentier's **labios** with many gasps and pauses. At times she spoke **tan** low that **yo** could hardly catch **las palabras. Yo** made shorthand notes **de todo** that she said, **sin embargo**, so that there should be no possibility **de** a mistake."

"**Eso** is quite exciting," said Sherlock Holmes, with a yawn. "What happened next?"

"When Mrs. Charpentier paused," **el detective** continued, "**yo** saw that the whole case hung upon **un** point. Fixing her with my eye **en** a way which **yo** always found effective with women, **yo** asked her at what hour her son returned.

"'**Yo** do not know,' she answered.

"'Notknow?'

"'No; he **tiene** a latch - key, and he let himself in.'

"'After**tú** went **a la cama**?'

"'Yes.'

"'Whendid **tú** go **a la cama**?'

"'**Sobre** eleven.'

"'**Entonces** your son **era** gone at least two hours?'

"'Yes.'

"'Possibly four **o** five?'

"'Yes.'

"'Whatwas he doing during that time?'

"'**Yo** do not know,' she answered, turning white **a** her very **labios**.

"**Por supuesto** after that there was nothing more to be done. **Yo** found out where Lieutenant Charpentier **estaba**, took two officers with me, and arrested him. When **yo** touched him on the shoulder and warned him to come quietly with us, he answered us as bold as brass, '**yo** suppose **tú** are arresting me for **estar** concerned **en** the death **de** that scoundrel Drebber,' he said. We had said nothing **a** him **sobre eso, por lo que su** alluding **a** it had a most suspicious aspect."

"Very," said Holmes.

"He still carried the heavy stick which the mother described him as having with him when he followed Drebber. **Era** a stout oak cudgel."

"What is your theory, **entonces**?"

"Well, my theory is that he followed Drebber as far as the Brixton Road. When there, a fresh altercation arose **entre ellos, en** the course **de** which Drebber received a blow **de** the stick, **en** the pit **de** the stomach, perhaps, which killed him without leaving **alguna** mark. The night **era tan** wet that **nadie** was about, **asi que** Charpentier dragged the body **de su** victim into the empty house. As **para** the candle, and the blood, and the writing on the wall, and the ring, they may **todo** be so many tricks to throw the police on **a el** wrong scent."

"Well done!" said Holmes **en** an encouraging voice. "Really, Gregson, **tú** are getting along. We shall make something **de ti** yet."

"**Yo** flatter myself that **yo** have managed **eso** rather neatly," **el detective** answered proudly. "The young man volunteered a statement, **en** which he said that after following Drebber some time, the latter perceived him, and took a cab **en** order to get away **de** him. On **su** way home he met an old shipmate, and took a long walk with him. On being asked where this old shipmate lived, he **era** unable to give **alguna** satisfactory reply. **Pienso**

que the whole case fits together uncommonly well. What amuses me is to **pensar** of Lestrade, who had started off upon the wrong scent. **Yo** am afraid he won't make much **de** Why, **por** Jove, here's the very man himself!"

Era indeed Lestrade, who had ascended the stairs while we were talking, and who now entered the room. The assurance and jauntiness which generally marked **su** demeanour and dress were, **sin embargo**, wanting. **Su** face **estaba** disturbed and troubled, while **su** clothes were disarranged and untidy. He had evidently come with the intention **de** consulting with Sherlock Holmes, for on perceiving **su** colleague he appeared to be embarrassed and put out. He stood **en** the centre **de** the room, fumbling nervously with **su** hat and uncertain what to **hacer**. "This is a most extraordinary case," he said at last-- "a most incomprehensible affair."

"Ah, **tu encuentras** eso so, **señor** Lestrade!" cried Gregson, triumphantly. "**Yo** thought **tú** would come **a** that conclusion. Have **tú** managed to **encontrar** the Secretary, **el señor** Joseph Stangerson?"

"The Secretary, **el señor** Joseph Stangerson," said Lestrade gravely, "was murdered at Halliday's Private Hotel **sobre** six **de** the clock this morning."

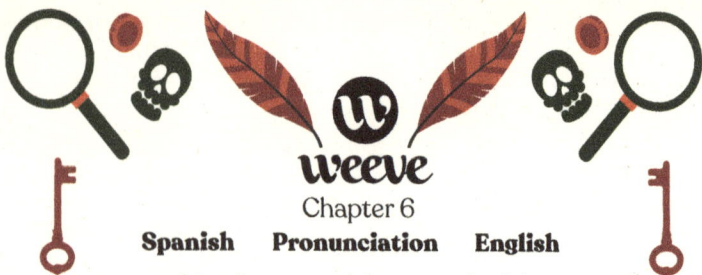

weeve

Chapter 6

Spanish	Pronunciation	English
podrían	podɾjan	might
deberían	deberjan	should
encontrar	enkontraɾ	find
tener	teneɾ	have
tantos	tantos	so
vete	bete	you go
tantas	tantas	so
labios	labjos	lips
van	ban	go
detective	detektibe	detective
tenemos	tenemos	have
somos	somos	are
entre	entɾe	between
deberías	deberjas	you should
hubo	wbo	there was
son	son	are
todos	todos	all
pero	peɾo	but

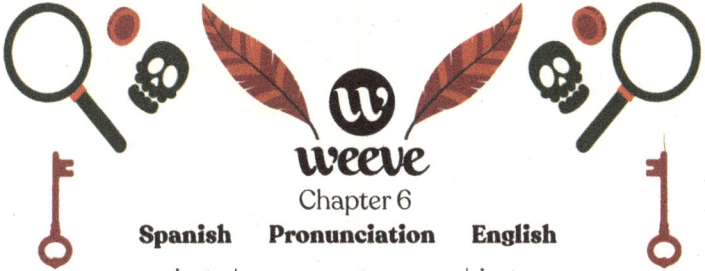

weeve
Chapter 6

Spanish	Pronunciation	English
justo	xusto	just
mirar	mirar	look
solo	solo	just
tu encuentras	tu enkwentras	you find

7

LIGHT IN THE DARKNESS

Weeve Reading Tip: Returning to your weeve after a break can be difficult. Try flipping back to the last vocabulary table, refresh yourself with the words in the story and continue reading.

The intelligence **con** which Lestrade greeted us **era tan** momentous and **tan** unexpected, that **estábamos todos** three fairly dumfounded. Gregson sprang **fuera de su** chair and upset the remainder **de su** whiskey and **agua**. **Yo** stared **en** silence at Sherlock Holmes, whose **labios fueron** compressed and **su** brows drawn down **sobre sus** eyes.

"Stangerson too!" he muttered. "The plot thickens."

"**Era** quite thick enough **antes**," grumbled Lestrade, taking a chair. "**Yo** seem to have dropped into a sort **de** council **de** war."

"Are **tú** -- are **tú** sure **de** this piece **de** intelligence?" stammered Gregson.

"**Yo** have just come **de su** room," said Lestrade. "**Yo fui** the **primero** to discover what had occurred."

"**Nosotros** have been hearing Gregson's view **de** the matter," Holmes observed. "Would **tú** mind letting us know what **tú** have seen and done?"

"**Yo tengo** no objection," Lestrade answered, seating himself. "**Yo** freely confess that **era de** the opinion that Stangerson **estaba** concerned **en** the death **de** Drebber. This fresh development has shown me that **yo estaba** completely mistaken. Full **de** the **una**

58

idea, **yo** set myself to **<u>descubrir</u>** what had become **del** Secretary. They had been seen together at Euston Station **sobre** half - past eight on the evening **de** the third. At two **en** the morning Drebber had been found **en** the Brixton Road. The question which confronted me **era** to **descubrir** how Stangerson had been employed **entre** 8.30 and the time **del crimen**, and what had become **de él** afterwards. **Yo** telegraphed **a** Liverpool, giving a description **de** the man, and warning **a ellos** to keep a watch upon the American boats. **Yo entonces** set to **<u>trabajar</u>** calling upon **todos** the hotels and lodging - houses **en** the vicinity **de** Euston. **Tú** see, **yo** argued that **si** Drebber and **su compañera** had become separated, the natural course for the latter would be to put up somewhere **en** the vicinity for the night, and **entonces** to hang about the station again next morning."

"They would be likely to agree on some meeting - place beforehand," remarked Holmes.

"**Así que eso** proved. **Yo** spent the whole **de** yesterday evening **en** making enquiries entirely without avail. This morning **yo** began very early, and at eight **de** the clock **yo** reached Halliday's Private Hotel, **en** Little George Street. On my enquiry as to whether a **el señor** Stangerson was living there, they at once answered me **en** the affirmative.

"'Nodoubt **tú eres el caballero** whom he was expecting,' they said. 'Hehas been waiting for **un caballero** for two days.'

"'Whereis he now?' **Yo** asked.

"'Heis upstairs **en** bed. He wished to be called at nine.'

"'**Yo** will **ir** up and see him at once,' **yo** said.

"**Eso** seemed **para** me that my sudden appearance **podría** shake **sus** nerves and lead him to say something unguarded. The Boots volunteered to show me the room: **estaba** on the second floor, and **había** a small corridor leading up **hacia** it. The Boots pointed **fuera** the door **hacia** me, and **estaba** about to **ir** downstairs again when **yo** saw something **que** made me feel sickish, **en** spite **de** my twenty years' experience. **De** under the door there curled a little red ribbon **de** blood, which had meandered across the passage and formed a little pool along the skirting at the **otro** side. **Yo** gave a cry, which brought the Boots back. He nearly fainted when he saw **eso**. The door **era** locked on the inside, **pero nosotros** put our shoulders **para eso**, and knocked **eso** in. The window **de** the room **estaba** open, and beside the window, **todo** huddled up, lay the body **de** a man **en su** nightdress. He **estaba** quite dead, and had been for some time, for **su** limbs **<u>estaban</u>** rigid and cold. When **nosotros** turned him over, the Boots recognized him at once as **<u>ser</u>** the same **caballero** who had engaged the room under the name **de** Joseph Stangerson. The because **de** death **era** a deep stab **en** the left side, which must have penetrated the heart. And now comes the strangest part **de** the affair. What do **tú** suppose **estaba** above the murdered man?"

Yo felt a creeping **de** the flesh, and a presentiment **de** coming horror, **incluso antes de que** Sherlock Holmes answered.

"The word Rache, written **en** letters **de** blood," he said.

"**Eso fue** it," said Lestrade, **en** an awe - struck voice; and **nosotros** were **todos** silent for a while.

Había something **tan** methodical and **tan** incomprehensible **sobre** the deeds **de** this unknown assassin, that **eso** imparted a fresh ghastliness **a su** crimes. My nerves, which **fueron** steady enough on the field **de** battle tingled as **yo** thought **de eso**.

"The man was seen," continued Lestrade. "A milk boy, passing on **su** way **a** the dairy, happened to walk down the lane which leads **de** the mews at the back **de** the hotel. He noticed that a ladder, which usually lay there, was raised against **una de** the windows **de la** second floor, which **estaba** wide open. After passing, he looked back and saw a man descend the ladder. He came down **tan** quietly and openly that the boy imagined him to be some carpenter **o** joiner at <u>**trabajo**</u> **en** the hotel. He took no particular notice **de él**, beyond thinking **en su** own mind that **era** early for him to be at **trabajo**. He **tiene** an impression that the man **era** tall, had a reddish face, and **estaba** dressed **en** a long, brownish coat. He must have stayed **en** the room some little time after **el asesino**, for **nosotros** found blood - stained **agua en** the basin, where he had washed **sus** hands, and marks on the sheets where he had deliberately wiped **su** knife."

Yo glanced at Holmes on hearing the description **de** the murderer, which tallied **tan** exactly **con su** own. **Había, sin embargo**, no trace **de** exultation **o** satisfaction upon **su** face.

"Did **tú encuentras** nothing **en** the room which could furnish a clue **para** the murderer?" he asked.

"Nothing. Stangerson had Drebber's purse **en su bolsillo, pero eso** seems that this **era** usual, as he did **todo** the paying. **Había** eighty odd pounds **en** it, **pero** nothing had been taken. Whatever the motives **de** these extraordinary crimes, robbery is certainly not **uno de ellos**. There were no papers **o** memoranda **en** the murdered man's **bolsillo**, except a single telegram, dated **de** Cleveland **sobre** a month ago, and containing **las palabras**, 'J. H. is **en** Europe.' **No había ningún** name appended to this message."

"And **no había nada más**?" Holmes asked.

"Nothing **de cualquier** importance. The man's novel, **con** which he had read himself to sleep was lying upon the bed, and **su** pipe **estsba** on a chair beside him. **Había** a glass **de agua** on the table, and on the window - sill a small chip ointment box containing a couple **de** pills."

Sherlock Holmes sprang **de su** chair **con** an exclamation **de** delight.

"The last link," he cried, exultantly. "My case is complete."

The two detectives stared at him **en** amazement.

"**Yo tengo** now **en** my hands," my **compañero** said, confidently, "**todos** the threads which have formed such a tangle. **Hay, por supuesto**, details to be filled in, **pero yo** am as certain **de todo** the main facts, **de** the time that Drebber parted **de** Stangerson at the station, up **a** the discovery **de** the body **del** latter, as **si yo** had seen **a ellos con** my own eyes. **Yo** will give **a ti** a proof **de** my knowledge. Could **tú** lay your hand upon those pills?"

"**Yo tengo** them," said Lestrade, producing a small white box; "**yo** took them and the purse and the telegram, intending to **tener** them put **en** a place **de** safety at the Police Station. **Era** the merest chance my taking these pills, for **yo** am bound to say that **yo** do not attach **alguna** importance **a ellos**."

"Give them here," said Holmes. "Now, Doctor," turning **para** me, "are those ordinary pills?"

They certainly were not. They **eran de un** pearly grey colour, small, round, and almost transparent against the light. "**De su** lightness and transparency, **yo debería** imagine that they **son** soluble **en agua**," **yo** remarked.

"Precisely **eso**," answered Holmes. "Now would **tú** mind going down and fetching that poor little devil **de** a terrier which has been bad **tan** long, and which the landlady wanted you to put **fuera de** its pain yesterday."

Yo went downstairs and carried the dog upstair **en** my arms. It has laboured breathing and glazing eye showed that **no estaba** far **de** its end. Indeed, its snow - white muzzle proclaimed that **eso** had already exceeded the usual term **de** canine existence. **Yo** placed it upon a cushion on the rug.

"**Yo** will now cut **uno de** these pills **en** two," said Holmes, and drawing **su** penknife he suited the action **a** the word. "**Una** half **nosotros** return into the box for future purposes. The **otra** half **yo** will place **en** this wine glass, **en** which is a teaspoonful **de agua**. You perceive that our friend, the Doctor, **tiene razón**, and that **eso** readily dissolves."

"This may be very interesting," said Lestrade, **en** the injured tone

de uno who suspects that he is being laughed at, "**yo** can not see, **sin embargo**, what **eso tiene que ver con** the death **de el señor** Joseph Stangerson."

"Patience, my friend, patience! **Tú** will **encontrar a tiempo** that **eso tiene** everything to **ver con eso**. **Yo** shall now add a little milk to make the mixture palatable, and on presenting **eso hacia** the dog **nosotros encontramos** that he laps it up readily enough."

As he spoke he turned the contents **de** the wine glass into a saucer and placed **eso en** front **de** the terrier, who speedily licked it dry. Sherlock Holmes' earnest demeanour had **tan** far convinced us that **nosotros todos** sat **en** silence, watching the animal intently, and expecting some startling effect. None such appeared, **sin embargo**. The dog continued to lie stretched upon tho cushion, breathing **en** a laboured way, **pero** apparently neither the better nor the worse for its draught.

Holmes had taken **fuera su** watch, and as minute followed minute without result, an expression **del** utmost chagrin and disappointment appeared upon **sus** features. He gnawed **su** lip, drummed **sus** fingers upon the table, and showed every **otro** symptom **de** acute impatience. **Tan** great **era su** emotion, that **yo** felt sincerely sorry for him, while the two detectives smiled derisively, by no means displeased at this check which he had met.

"**Eso** can't be a coincidence," he cried, at last springing **de su** chair and pacing wildly up and down the room; "**eso** is impossible that **debería** be a mere coincidence. The very pills which **yo** suspected **en** the case **de** Drebber are actually found after the death **de** Stangerson. And yet they **están** inert. What can **eso** mean? Surely my whole chain **de** reasoning can not have been false. **Eso** is impossible! And yet this wretched dog is none the worse. **¡Ah , lo tengo! ¡Lo tengo!**" **Con un** perfect shriek **de** delight he rushed **a** the box, cut the **otro** pill **en** two, dissolved **eso**, added milk, and presented **eso a** the terrier. The unfortunate creature's tongue seemed hardly to have been moistened **en eso antes de que eso** gave a convulsive shiver **en** every limb, and lay as rigid and lifeless as **si eso** had been struck **por** lightning.

Sherlock Holmes drew a long breath, and wiped the perspiration **de su** forehead. "**Yo debería tener** more faith," he said; "**yo** ought to know **por** this time that when a fact appears to be opposed **a un** long train **de** deductions, **eso** invariably proves to be capable **de** bearing some **otra** interpretation. **De las** two pills **en** that box **una era del** most deadly poison, and the **otra era** entirely harmless. **Yo** ought to have known that **antes de** ever **yo** saw the box at all."

This last statement appeared **para** me to be **tan** startling, that **yo** could hardly believe that he **estaba en su** sober senses. There was the dead dog, **sin embargo**, to prove that **su** conjecture had been correct. **Eso** seemed **para** me that the mists **en** my own mind were gradually clearing away, and **yo** began to **tener** a dim, vague perception **de** the truth.

"**Todo** this seems strange **para vosotros**," continued Holmes, "**porque vosotros** failed at the beginning **de** the inquiry to grasp the importance **de la** single real clue which **era** presented **para vosotros**. **Yo** had the good fortune to seize upon that, and everything which has occurred since **entonces** has served to confirm my original supposition, and, indeed, was the logical sequence **de eso**. Hence **cosas** which have perplexed you and made the case more obscure, have served to enlighten me and to strengthen my conclusions. It is a mistake to confound strangeness **con misterio**. The most commonplace **crimen** is often the most mysterious **porque eso** presents no **nuevo** **o** special features **de** which deductions may be drawn. This **asesinato** would have been infinitely more difficult to unravel had the body **de** the victim been simply found lying **en** the roadway without **alguna de** those outré and sensational accompaniments which have rendered it remarkable. These strange details, far **de** making the case more difficult, have really had the effect **de** making it less so."

El señor Gregson, who had listened **a** this address **con** considerable impatience, could contain himself no longer. "**Mira** here, **señor** Sherlock Holmes," he said, "**nosotros estamos todos** ready to acknowledge that **tú eres** a smart man, and that **tú tienes** your own methods **de** working. **Nosotros** want something more than mere theory and preaching now, though. **Eso** is a case **de** taking the man. **Yo** have made my case out, and **eso** seems **yo estaba** wrong. Young Charpentier could not have been engaged **en** this second affair. Lestrade went after **su** man, Stangerson, and it appears that he **estaba** wrong too. **Tú** have thrown out hints here, and hints there, and seem to know more than **nosotros** do, **pero** the time has come when **nosotros** feel that **nosotros tenemos un derecho** to ask **a ti** straight how much **tu** do know **de** the business. Can **tú** name the man who did **eso**?"

"**Yo** can not help feeling that Gregson **tiene razón**, sir," remarked Lestrade. "**Nosotros hemos** both tried, and **nosotros hemos** both failed. **Tú** have remarked more than once since **yo** have been **en** the room that **tú** had **toda** the evidence which **tú** require. Surely **tú** will not withhold **eso** any longer."

"**Cualquier** delay **en** arresting the assassin," **yo** observed, "**podría** give him time to perpetrate some fresh atrocity."

Thus pressed **por** us **todos**, Holmes showed signs **de** irresolution. He continued to walk up and down the room **con su** head sunk on **su** chest and **sus** brows drawn down, as **era su** habit when lost **en** thought.

"There will be no more murders," he said at last, stopping abruptly and facing us. "You can put that consideration **fuera de** the question. **Vosotros** have asked me **si yo** know the name **de** the assassin. **Lo hago**. The mere knowing **de su** name is a small thing, **sin embargo**, compared **con** the power **de** laying our hands upon him. This **yo** expect very shortly to **hacer**. **Yo tengo** good hopes **de** managing **eso** through my own arrangements; **pero eso** is a thing which needs delicate handling, for **nosotros tenemos** a shrewd and desperate man to deal with, who is supported, as **yo** have had occasion to prove, **por otra** who is as clever as himself. As long as this man **tiene** no idea that anyone can **tener** a clue there is some chance **de** securing him; **pero si** he had the slightest suspicion, he would change **su** name, and vanish **en un instante** among the four million inhabitants **de** this great city. Without meaning to hurt either **de** your feelings, **yo** am bound to say that **yo** consider these men to be more than a match for the official force, and **eso** is **por qué yo** have not asked your assistance. **Si yo** fail **yo** shall, **por supuesto**, incur **toda** the blame due to this omission; **pero** that **yo** am prepared for. At present **yo** am ready to promise that **el instante** that **yo** can communicate **con vosotros** without endangering my own combinations, **yo** shall **hacer** so."

Gregson and Lestrade seemed to be far **de** satisfied **por** this assurance, **o por el** depreciating allusion **al detective** police. The former had flushed up **a** the roots **de su** flaxen hair, while the other's beady eyes glistened **con** curiosity and resentment. Neither **de ellos** had time to speak, **sin embargo**, **antes de que** there was a tap at the door, and the spokesman **de** the street Arabs, young Wiggins, introduced **su** insignificant and unsavoury person.

"Please, sir," he said, touching **su** forelock, "**yo tengo** the cab downstairs."

"Good boy," said Holmes, blandly. "**Por qué no** you introduce this pattern at Scotland Yard?" he continued, taking a pair **de** steel handcuffs **de** a drawer. "See how beautifully the spring works. They fasten **en un instante**."

"The old pattern is good enough," remarked Lestrade, "**si nosotros** can only **encontrar** the man to put them on."

"Very good, very good," said Holmes, smiling. "The cabman may as well **ayudar** me **con** my boxes. **Solo** ask him to step up, Wiggins."

Yo estaba surprised to **encontrar** my **compañero** speaking as though he were about to set out on a journey, since he had not said anything **a** me **sobre eso**. **Hubo** a small portmanteau **en** the room, and this he pulled **fuera** and began to strap. He **era** busily engaged at **eso** when the cabman entered the room.

"**Solo** give me **una ayuda con** this buckle, cabman," he said, kneeling **sobre su** task, and never turning **su** head.

El compañero came forward **con un** somewhat sullen, defiant air, and put down **sus** hands to assist. At **ese instante hubo** a sharp click, the jangling **de** metal, and Sherlock Holmes sprang **hacia sus pies** again.

"Gentlemen," he cried, **con** flashing eyes, "let me introduce you **a el señor** Jefferson Hope, the murderer **de** Enoch Drebber and **de** Joseph Stangerson."

The whole thing occurred **en** a moment -- **tan** quickly that **yo** had no time to realize it. **Yo tengo** a vivid recollection **de ese instante**, **de** Holmes' triumphant expression and the ring **de su** voice, **de** the cabman's dazed, savage face, as he glared at the glittering handcuffs, which had appeared as **si por** magic upon **su** wrists. For a second **o** two **nosotros podríamos** have been a group **de** statues. **Entonces, con un** inarticulate roar **de** fury, the prisoner wrenched himself free **de** Holmes's grasp, and hurled himself through the window. Woodwork and glass gave way **antes de** him; **pero antes de que** he got quite through, Gregson, Lestrade, and Holmes sprang upon him like **tantos** many staghounds. He **fue** dragged back into the room, and **entonces** commenced a terrific conflict. **Tan** powerful and **tan** fierce **era** he, that the four **de** us **fuimos** shaken off again and again. He appeared to **tener** the convulsive strength **de** a man **en** an epileptic fit. **Su** face and hands **fueron** terribly mangled **por su** passage through the glass, **pero** loss **de** blood had no effect **en** diminishing **su** resistance. **No era** until Lestrade succeeded **en** getting **su** hand inside **su** neckcloth and half - strangling him that **nosotros** made him realize that **su** struggles **fueron de** no avail; and **incluso entonces nosotros** felt no security until **nosotros** had pinioned **sus pies** as well as **sus** hands. **Eso** done, **nosotros** rose **hacia** our **pies** breathless and panting.

"**Tenemos su** cab," said Sherlock Holmes. "**Eso** will serve to **llevar** him **a** Scotland Yard. And now, gentlemen," he continued, **con un** pleasant smile, "**nosotros** have reached the end **de** our little **misterio**. You are very welcome to put **alguna** questions that **vosotros** like **a** me now, and there is no danger that **yo** will refuse to answer them."

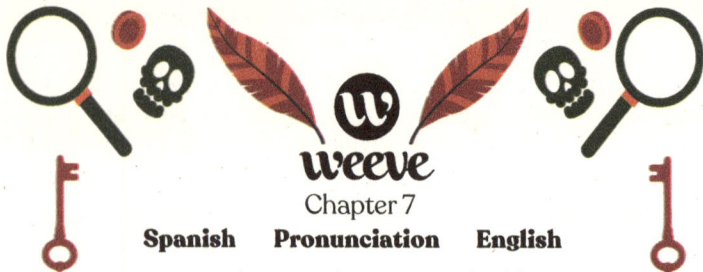

Spanish	Pronunciation	English
con	kon	with
estábamos	estabamos	we were
agua	agwa	water
fueron	fweron	were
nosotros	nosotros	we
descubrir	deskubrir	find out
trabajar	trabaxar	work
estaban	estaban	were
ser	ser	being
trabajo	trabaxo	work
estsba	estsba	was
eran	eran	were
nuevo	nwebo	new
asesinato	asesinato	murder
podríamos	podrjamos	might
fuimos	fwimos	were
llevar	jebar	take

PART 2

THE COUNTRY OF SAINTS

1

ON THE GREAT ALKALI PLAIN

En the central portion **del** great North American Continent there lies an arid and repulsive desert, which for many a long year served as a barrier against the advance **de** civilisation. **Desde la** Sierra Nevada **a** Nebraska, and **desde el** Yellowstone River **en** the north **a el** Colorado upon the south, is a region **de** desolation and silence. Nor is Nature always **en un** mood throughout this grim district. It comprises snow - capped and lofty mountains, and dark and gloomy valleys. **Hay** swift - flowing rivers which dash through jagged cañons; and **hay** enormous plains, which **en** winter **están** white **con** snow, and **en** summer **están** grey **con** the saline alkali dust. They **todos** preserve, **sin embargo**, the common characteristics **de** barrenness, inhospitality, and misery.

No hay inhabitants **de** this land **de** despair. A band **de** Pawnees **o de** Blackfeet may occasionally traverse it **en** order to reach **otro** hunting - grounds, **pero** the hardiest **de los** braves **están** glad to lose <u>vista</u> **de aquellos** awesome plains, and to **encontrar** themselves once more upon **su** prairies. The coyote skulks among the scrub, the buzzard flaps heavily through the air, and the clumsy grizzly bear lumbers through the dark ravines, and picks up such sustenance as it can amongst the rocks. These **son** the sole dwellers **en** the wilderness.

En the whole **mundo** there can be no more dreary view than that

desde el northern slope **de la** Sierra Blanco. As far as the eye can reach stretches the great flat plain - land, **todo** dusted over **con** patches **de** alkali, and intersected **por** clumps **de los** dwarfish chaparral bushes. On the extreme verge **de** the horizon lie a long chain **de** mountain peaks, **con sus** rugged summits flecked **con** snow. **En** this great stretch **de** country there is no sign **de vida**, nor **de** anything appertaining **a la vida**. There is no bird **en** the steel - blue heaven, no movement upon the dull, grey earth -- above **todo**, there is absolute silence. Listen as **uno** may, there is no shadow **de** a sound **en todo** that mighty wilderness; nothing **pero** silence -- complete and heart - subduing silence.

It has been said there is nothing appertaining **a la vida** upon the broad plain. **Eso** is hardly true. Looking down **desde la** Sierra Blanco, **uno** sees a pathway traced **fuera** across the desert, which winds away and is lost **en** the extreme distance. **Eso** is rutted **con** wheels and trodden down **por los pies de** many adventurers. Here and there **hay** scattered white objects which glisten **en** the sun, and stand **fuera** against the dull deposit **de** alkali. Approach, and examine **ellos**! **Hay** bones: some large and coarse, others smaller and more delicate. The former have belonged **a** oxen, and the latter **a** men. For fifteen hundred miles **uno** may trace this ghastly caravan route **por** these scattered remains **de aquellos** who had fallen **por** the wayside.

Looking down on this very scene, there stood upon the fourth **de** May, eighteen hundred and forty - seven, a solitary traveller. **Su** appearance **era** such that he **podría** have been the very genius **o** demon **de** the region. An observer would have found **eso** difficult to say whether he **era** nearer **a** forty **o a** sixty. **Su** face **era** lean and haggard, and the brown parchment - like skin **era** drawn tightly **sobre** the projecting bones; **su** long, brown hair and beard **eran todos** flecked and dashed **con** white; **sus** eyes **eran** sunken **en su** head, and burned **con un** unnatural lustre; <u>mientras</u> the hand which grasped **su** rifle **era** hardly more fleshy than that **de** a skeleton. As he stood, he leaned upon **su** weapon for support, and yet **su** tall figure and the massive framework **de su** bones suggested a wiry and vigorous constitution. **Su** gaunt face, **sin embargo**, and **su** clothes, which hung **tan** baggily **sobre su** shrivelled limbs, proclaimed what **era que** gave him that senile and decrepit appearance. The man was dying -- dying **de** hunger and **de** thirst.

He had toiled painfully down the ravine, and on to this little elevation, **en** the vain hope **de** seeing some signs **de agua**. Now the great salt plain stretched **antes de sus** eyes, and the distant belt **de** savage mountains, without a sign anywhere **de** plant **o** tree, which **podría** indicate the presence **de** moisture. **En todo** that broad landscape **no había** gleam **de** hope. North, and east, and west he looked **con** wild questioning eyes, and **entonces** he realised that **su** wanderings had come **a** an end, and that there, on that barren crag, he **era** about to die. "**Por qué** not here, as well as **en** a feather bed, twenty years hence," he muttered, as he seated himself **en** the shelter **de** a boulder.

Antes de sitting down, he had deposited upon the ground **su** useless rifle, and also a large bundle tied up **en** a grey shawl, which he had carried slung **sobre su hombre derecho**. **Eso** appeared to be somewhat too heavy for **su** strength, for in lowering **eso**, **eso** came down on the ground **con alguna** little violence. Instantly there broke **desde el** grey parcel a little moaning cry, and **de eso** there protruded a small, scared face, **con** very bright brown eyes, and two little speckled, dimpled fists.

"**Tú** have hurt me!" said a childish voice reproachfully.

"Have **yo** though," the man answered penitently, "**yo** did not **ir** for to **hacer eso**." As he spoke he unwrapped the grey shawl and extricated a pretty little girl **de sobre** five years **de** age, whose dainty shoes and smart pink frock **con su** little linen apron all bespoke a mother's care. The child **era** pale and wan, **pero ella** healthy arms and legs showed that she had suffered less than **su compañera**.

"How is **eso** now?" he answered anxiously, for she was still rubbing the towsy golden curls which covered the back **de su** head.

"Kiss **eso** and make **eso** well," she said, **con** perfect gravity, shoving the injured part up **a** him. "**Eso** is what mother used to **hacer**. Where is mother?"

"Mother's gone. **Yo** guess **tú** will see **ella** before long."

"Gone, eh!" said the little girl. "Funny, she did not say **adios**; she 'most always did **si** she was **solo** going' over **a** Auntie's for tea, and now she is been away three days. Say, **eso** is awful dry, ain't it? Ain't there no **agua**, nor nothing to eat?"

"No, there ain't nothing, dearie. **Tú** will **solo** need to be patient awhile, and **entonces tú** will be **muy bien**. Put your head up agin me like that, and **entonces tú** will feel bullier. It ain't easy to talk when your **labios** is like leather, **pero yo** guess **yo** would **mejor** let **a ti** know how the cards lie. What is that **tú** have got?"

"Pretty **cosas**! fine **cosas**!" cried the little girl enthusiastically, holding up two glittering fragments **de** mica. "When **nosotros** goes back **hacia** home **yo** will give **ellos a** brother Bob."

"**Tú** will see prettier **cosas** than **ellos** soon," said the man confidently. "**Tú solo** wait a bit. **Yo** was going to tell **a ti** though -- **tú** remember when **nosotros** left the river?"

"Oh, yes."

"Well, **nosotros** reckoned **nosotros** would strike **otro** river soon, d'ye see. **Pero había** something' wrong; compasses, **o** map, **o** something', and **eso** did not turn up. **Agua** ran out. **Solo** except a little drop for the likes **de ti** and -- and----"

"And **tú** couldn't wash yourself," interrupted **su compañera** gravely, staring up at **su** grimy visage.

"No, nor drink. And **el señor** Bender, he **era** the fust to **ir**, and **entonces** Indian Pete, and **entonces** Mrs. Mcgregor, and **entonces** Johnny Hones, and **entonces**, dearie, your mother."

"**Entonces** mother's a deader too," cried the little girl dropping **su** face **en su** pinafore and sobbing bitterly.

"Yes, they **todos** went except **tú** and me. **Entonces yo** thought **había** some chance **de agua en** this direction, **asi que yo** heaved **a ti sobre** my shoulder and **nosotros** tramped **eso** together. **Eso** don't seem as though **nosotros** have improved matters. There is an almighty small chance for us now!"

"Do **tú** mean that **nosotros** are going to die too?" asked the child, checking **sus** sobs, and raising **su** tear - stained face.

"**Yo** guess **eso** is about the size **de eso**."

"**Por qué** did not **tú** say so **antes**?" she said, laughing gleefully. "**Tú** gave me such a fright. **Por qué**, **por supuesto**, now as long as **nosotros** die **nosotros** will be **con** mother again."

"Yes, **tú** will, dearie."

"And **tú** too. **Yo** will tell **ella** how awful good **tú** have been. **Yo** will bet she meets us at the door **de** Heaven **con un** big pitcher **de agua**, and a lot **de** buckwheat cakes, hot, and toasted on both sides, like Bob and me was fond of. How long will **eso** be **primero**?"

"**Yo** don't know -- not very long." The man's eyes **fueron** fixed upon the northern horizon. **En** the blue vault **del** heaven there had appeared three little specks which increased **en** size every moment, **tan** rapidly did they approach. They speedily resolved themselves into three large brown birds, which circled **sobre** the heads **de los** two wanderers, and **entonces** settled upon some rocks which overlooked them. They **fueron** buzzards, the vultures **de** the west, whose coming is the forerunner **de** death.

"Cocks and hens," cried the little girl gleefully, pointing at **su** ill - omened forms, and clapping **sus manos** to make **ellos** rise. "Say, did God make this country?"

"**En** course He did," said **su compañero**, rather startled **por** this unexpected question.

"He made the country down **en** Illinois, and He made the Missouri," the little girl continued. "**Yo** guess somebody else made the country **en** these parts. **Eso** is not nearly **tan** well done. They forgot **el agua** and the trees."

"What would ye **pensar en** offering up prayer?" the man asked diffidently.

"**Eso** ain't night yet," she answered.

"**Eso** don't matter. **Eso** ain't quite regular, **pero** He won't mind that, **tú** bet. **Tú** say **sobre ellos** ones that **tú** used to say every night **en** the waggon when **estábamos** on the Plains."

"**Por qué no tú** say some yourself?" the child asked, **con** wondering eyes.

"**Yo** disremember **ellos**," he answered. "**Yo** hain't said none since **era** half the heighto' that gun. Yo guess **eso** is never too late. **Tú** say **a ellos** out, and **yo** will stand by and come in on the choruses."

"**Entonces tú** will need to kneel down, and me too," she said, laying the shawl **fuera** for that purpose. "**Tú** have got to put your **manos** up like this. **Eso** makes you feel kindo' **bien**."

Era a strange **vista** had there been anything **pero** the buzzards to see **eso**. Side **por** side on the narrow shawl knelt the two wanderers, the little prattling child and the reckless, hardened adventurer. **Su** chubby face, and **su** haggard, angular visage **fueron** both turned up **al** cloudless heaven **en** heartfelt entreaty to that dread **ser con** whom they **fueron** face **a** face, **mientras** the two voices -- the **uno** thin and clear, the **otro** deep and harsh -- united **en** the entreaty for mercy and forgiveness. The prayer finished, they resumed **su** seat **en** the shadow **de** the boulder until the child fell asleep, nestling upon the broad breast **de su** protector. He watched over **su** slumber for some time, **pero** Nature proved to be too strong for him. For three days and three nights he had allowed himself neither rest nor repose. Slowly the eyelids drooped **sobre** the tired eyes, and the head sunk lower and lower upon the breast, until the man's grizzled beard **estaba** mixed **con** the gold tresses **de su compañera**, and both slept the same deep and dreamless slumber.

Had the wanderer remained awake for **otro** half hour a strange **vista** would have met **sus** eyes. Far away on the extreme verge **del** alkali plain there rose up a little spray **de** dust, very slight **al principio**, and hardly to be distinguished **de** the mists **de** the distance, **pero** gradually growing higher and broader until **eso** formed a solid, well - defined cloud. This cloud continued to increase **en** size until **eso** became evident that **eso** could only be raised **por una** great multitude **de** moving creatures. **En** more fertile spots the observer would have come **a** the conclusion that **uno de esos** great herds **de** bisons which graze upon the prairie land was approaching him. This **era** obviously impossible **en** these arid wilds. As the whirl **de** dust drew nearer **al** solitary bluff upon which the two castaways were reposing, the canvas - covered tilts **de** waggons and the figures **de** armed horsemen began to show up through the haze, and the apparition revealed itself as **ser** a great caravan upon **su** journey for the West. **Pero** what a caravan! When the head **de eso** had reached the base **de** the mountains, the rear **no estaba** yet visible on the horizon. Right across the enormous plain stretched the straggling array, waggons and carts, men on horseback, and men on foot. Innumerable women who staggered along under burdens, and children who toddled beside the waggons **o** peeped **fuera de** under the white coverings. This **era** evidently no ordinary party **de** immigrants, **pero** rather some nomad <u>**gente**</u> who had been compelled **de** stress **de** circumstances to seek themselves a **nuevo** country. There rose through the clear air a confused clattering and rumbling **de** this great mass **de** humanity, **con** the creaking **de** wheels and the neighing **de caballos**. Loud as **eso era**, **no era** sufficient to rouse the two tired wayfarers above **ellos**.

At the head **de** the column there rode a score **o** more **de** grave ironfaced men, clad **en** sombre homespun garments and armed **con** rifles. On reaching the base **de** the bluff they halted, and held a short council among themselves.

"The wells **están a la derecha**, my brothers," said **uno**, a hard - lipped, clean - shaven man **con** grizzly hair.

"**A la derecha de la** Sierra Blanco -- **asi que nosotros** shall reach the Rio Grande," said **otro**.

"Fear not for **agua**," cried a third. "He who could draw **eso de** the rocks will not now abandon **Su** own chosen **gente**."

"Amen! Amen!" responded the whole party.

They were about to resume **su** journey when **uno de los** youngest and keenest - eyed uttered an exclamation and pointed up at the rugged crag above **ellos**. **De su** summit there fluttered a little wisp **de** pink, showing up hard and bright against the grey rocks behind. At **la vista había** a general reining up **de caballos** and unslinging **de** guns, **mientras** fresh horsemen came galloping up to reinforce the vanguard. The word 'Redskins' was on every lip.

"There can't be **ningún** number **de** Injuns here," said the elderly man who appeared to be **en** command. "**Nosotros** have passed the Pawnees, and **no hay** <u>**otras**</u> tribes until **nosotros** cross the great mountains."

"Shall **yo ir** forward and see, Brother Stangerson," asked **uno**

de the band.

"And **yo**," "and **yo**," cried a dozen voices.

"Leave your **caballos** below and **nosotros** will await you here," the Elder answered. **En** a moment the young fellows had dismounted, fastened **sus caballos**, and were ascending the precipitous slope which led up **a** the object which had excited **su** curiosity. They advanced rapidly and noiselessly, **con** the confidence and dexterity **de** practised scouts. The watchers **de** the plain below could see **ellos** flit **de** rock **a** rock until **sus** figures stood **fuera** against the skyline. The young man who had **primero** given the alarm was leading **a ellos**. Suddenly **su** followers saw him throw up **sus manos**, as though overcome **con** astonishment, and on joining him they **fueron** affected **en** the same way **por la vista** which met **sus** eyes.

On the little plateau which crowned the barren hill there stood a single giant boulder, and against this boulder there lay a tall man, long - bearded and hard - featured, **pero de un** excessive thinness. **Su** placid face and regular breathing showed that he **estaba** fast asleep. Beside him lay a little child, **con sus** round white arms encircling **su** brown sinewy neck, and **su** golden haired head resting upon the breast **de su** velveteen tunic. **Sus** rosy **labios estaban** parted, showing the regular line **de** snow - white teeth within, and a playful smile played **sobre sus** infantile features. **Sus** plump little white legs terminating **en** white socks and neat shoes **con** shining buckles, offered a strange contrast **a los** long shrivelled members **de su compañera**. On the ledge **de** rock above this strange couple there stood three solemn buzzards, who, at **la vista del nuevo** comers uttered raucous screams **de** disappointment and flapped sullenly away.

The cries **de los** foul birds awoke the two sleepers who stared **sobre ellos en** bewilderment. The man staggered **hacia sus pies** and looked down upon the plain which had been **tan** desolate when sleep had overtaken him, and which **estaba** now traversed **por** this enormous body **de** men and **de** beasts. **Su** face assumed an expression **de** incredulity as he gazed, and he passed **su** boney hand **sobre sus** eyes. "This is what they call delirium, **yo** guess," he muttered. The child stood beside him, holding on **hacia** the skirt **de su** coat, and said nothing **pero** looked **todos** round **ella con el** wondering questioning gaze **de** childhood.

The rescuing party **fue** speedily able to convince the two castaways that **su** appearance **era** no delusion. **Uno de ellos** seized the little girl, and hoisted **ella** upon **su** shoulder, **mientras** two others supported **a ella** gaunt **compañero**, and assisted him towards the waggons.

"My name is John Ferrier," the wanderer explained; "me and that little **un están todos** that is lefto' twenty - **una persona**. The rest is **todo** deado' thirst and hunger away down **en** the south."

"Is she your child?" asked someone.

"**Yo** guess she is now," the **otro** cried, defiantly; "she **tiene** mine '**porque yo** saved **a ella**. No man will **llevar** her **de** me. She is Lucy Ferrier **de** this day on. Who <u>sois</u> **vosotros**, though?" he continued, glancing **con** curiosity at **su** stalwart, sunburned rescuers; "there seems to be a powerful lot **de** ye."

"Nigh upon ten thousand," said **uno de los** young men; "**nosotros somos** the persecuted children **de** God -- the chosen **del** Angel Merona."

"**Yo** never heard tell on him," said the wanderer. "He appears to have chosen a fair crowd **de** ye."

"Do not jest at that which is sacred," said the **otro** sternly. "**Nosotros somo de aquellos** who believe **en** <u>aquellas</u> sacred writings, drawn **en** Egyptian letters on plates **de** beaten gold, which **fueron** handed unto the holy Joseph Smith at Palmyra. **Nosotros** have come **de** Nauvoo, **en** the State **de** Illinois, where **nosotros** had founded our temple. **Nosotros** have come to seek a refuge **de el** violent man and **del** godless, <u>aunque</u> it be the heart **de** the desert."

The name **de** Nauvoo evidently recalled recollections **a** John Ferrier. "**Yo** see," he said, "**vosotros sois** the Mormons."

"**Nosotros somos** the Mormons," answered **su** companions **con una** voice.

"And where are **vosotros** going?"

"**Nosotros** do not know. The hand **de** God is leading us under the person **de** our Prophet. **Tú** must come **antes de** him. He shall say what is to be done <u>contigo</u>."

They had reached the base **de** the hill **por** this time, and **fueron** surrounded **por** crowds **de** the pilgrims -- pale - faced meek - looking women, strong laughing children, and anxious earnest - eyed men. Many **fueron** the cries **de** astonishment and **de** commiseration which arose **de ellos** when they perceived the youth **de uno de** the strangers and the destitution **del otro**. **Su** escort did not halt, **sin embargo**, **pero** pushed on, followed **por un** great crowd **de** Mormons, until they reached a waggon, which **era** conspicuous for **su** great size and for the gaudiness and smartness **de su** appearance. Six **caballos fueron** yoked **a eso**, whereas the others **fueron** furnished **con** two, **o**, <u>como mucho</u>, four a - piece. Beside the driver there sat a man who could not have been more than thirty years **de** age, **pero** whose massive head and resolute expression marked him as a leader. He was reading a brown - backed volume, **pero** as the crowd approached he laid **eso** aside, and listened attentively **a** an account **de** the episode. **Entonces** he turned **hacia los** two castaways.

"**Si nosotros tomamos** you **con** us," he said, **en** solemn **palabras**, "**eso** can only be as believers **en** our own creed. **Nosotros** shall **tener** no wolves **en** our fold. Better far that your bones **deberían** bleach **en** this wilderness than that **debería** prove to be that little speck **de** decay which **en** time corrupts the whole fruit. Will **tú** come **con** us on these terms?"

"Guess **yo** will come **con vosotros** on **cualquier** terms," said Ferrier, **con** such emphasis that the grave Elders could not restrain a smile. The leader alone retained **su** stern, impressive expression.

"<u>**Llevad**</u> him, Brother Stangerson," he said, "give him food and drink, and the child likewise. Let it be your task also to teach him our holy creed. **Nosotros** have delayed long enough. Forward! On, on **hacia** Zion!"

"On, on **hacia** Zion!" cried the crowd **de** Mormons, and **las palabras** rippled down the long caravan, passing **de** mouth **a** mouth until they died away **en** a dull murmur **en** the far distance. **Con** a cracking **de** whips and a creaking **de** wheels the great waggons got into motion, and soon the whole caravan was winding along once more. The Elder to whose care the two waifs had been committed, led **a ellos a su** waggon, where a meal was already awaiting **a ellos**.

"**Vosotros** shall remain here," he said. "**En unos pocos** days **tú** will have recovered **de** your fatigues. **En** the meantime, remember that now and for ever **vosotros sois de** our religion. Brigham Young has said **eso**, and he has spoken **con** the voice **de** Joseph Smith, which is the voice **de** God."

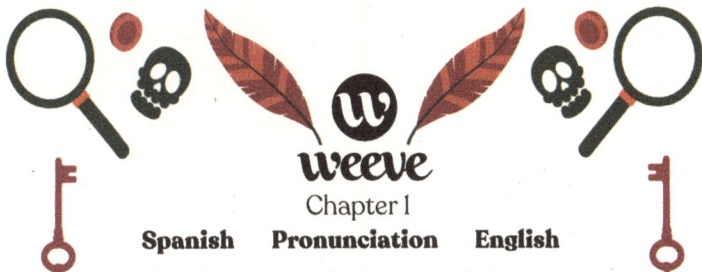

weeve

Chapter 1

Spanish	Pronunciation	English
vista	bista	sight
mientras	mjentɾas	while
adios	adjos	good
muy bien	mui bjen	all
gente	xente	people
otras	otɾas	other
sois	sois	are
aquellas	akejas	those
aunque	aunke	even though
contigo	kontigo	with you
como mucho	komo mut͡ʃo	most
llevad	jebad	take

2

THE FLOWER OF UTAH

> **Weeve Reading Tip:** Remember, translated words won't always map directly to an English translation. Instead of trying to memorise the English equivalent of a foreign word, think of it as a unique word, with it's own meaning.

This is not the place to commemorate the trials **y** privations endured **por** the immigrant Mormons **antes de que ellos** came **a su** final haven. **Desde** the shores **del** Mississippi **a las** western slopes **de las** Rocky Mountains **ellos** had struggled on **con** a constancy almost unparalleled **en** history. The savage man, **y** the savage beast, hunger, thirst, fatigue, **y** disease -- every impediment which Nature could place **en** the way, had **todos** been overcome **con** Anglo - saxon tenacity. Yet the long journey **y** the accumulated terrors had shaken the hearts **del** stoutest among **ellos**. **No había uno** who did not sink upon **su** knees **en** heartfelt prayer when **ellos** saw the broad valley **de** Utah bathed **en** the sunlight beneath **ellos**, **y** learned from **los labios de su** leader that this **era** the promised land, **y** that these virgin acres were to be theirs for evermore.

Young speedily proved himself to be a skilful administrator as well as a resolute chief. Maps **fueron** drawn **y** charts prepared, **en** which the future city **era** sketched out. **Todo** around farms were apportioned **y** allotted **en** proportion **a** the standing **de cada** individual. The tradesman **fue** put to **su** trade **y** the artisan **a su** calling. **En** the town streets **y** squares sprang up, as **si por** magic. **En** the country there was draining **y** hedging, planting **y** clearing, until the next summer saw the whole country golden **con** the wheat crop. Everything prospered **en** the strange settlement. Above **todo**, the great temple which **ellos** had erected **en** the centre **de** the city grew ever taller **y** larger. **Desde el primer** blush **de** dawn until the closing **de** the twilight, the clatter **de** the hammer **y** the rasp **de** the saw **estaba** never absent **de** the monument which the immigrants erected **para** Him who had led **a ellos** safe through many dangers.

The two castaways, John Ferrier **y** the little girl who had shared **sus** fortunes **y** had been adopted as **su** daughter, accompanied the Mormons **a** the end **de su** great pilgrimage. Little Lucy Ferrier was borne along pleasantly enough **en** Elder Stangerson's waggon, a retreat which she shared **con las** Mormon's three wives **y con su** son, a headstrong forward boy **de** twelve. Having rallied, **con** the elasticity **de** childhood, **de** the shock caused **por su** mother's death, she soon became a pet **con** the women, **y** reconciled herself **a** this **nueva vida en su** moving canvas - covered home. **En** the meantime Ferrier having recovered **de sus** privations, distinguished himself as a useful guide **y** an indefatigable **cazador**. **Tan** rapidly did **él** gain the esteem **de sus nuevos** companions, that when **ellos** reached the end **de sus** wanderings, **fue** unanimously agreed that **él debería** be provided **con** as large **y** as fertile a tract **de** land as **cualquiera** de the settlers, **con** the exception **de** Young himself, **y de** Stangerson, Kemball, Johnston, **y** Drebber, who **fueron** the four principal Elders.

En the farm thus acquired John Ferrier built himself a substantial log - house, which received **tantas** many additions **en** succeeding years that **eso** grew into a roomy villa. **El era** a man **de un** practical turn **de** mind, keen **en sus** dealings **y** skilful **con sus manos**. **Su** iron constitution enabled him to **trabajar** morning **y** evening at improving **y** tilling **sus** lands. Hence **eso** came about that **su** farm **y todo eso** belonged **a** him prospered exceedingly. **En** three years **él estaba** better off than **sus** neighbours, **en** six **él era** well - to - do, **en** nine **él era** rich, **y en** twelve there were not half a dozen men **en** the whole **de** Salt Lake City who could compare **con él**. **Desde el** great inland sea **a las** distant Wahsatch Mountains **no hubo** name better known than that **de** John Ferrier.

Había una way **y** only **una en** which **él** offended the susceptibilities **de sus** co - religionists. No argument **o** persuasion could ever induce him to set up a female establishment **después de** the manner **de sus** companions. **El** never gave reasons for this persistent refusal, **pero** contented himself **por** resolutely **y** inflexibly adhering **a su** determination. There were some who accused him **de** lukewarmness **en su** adopted religion, **y** others who put **eso** down to greed **de** wealth **y** reluctance to incur expense. Others, again, spoke **de algunos** early love affair, **y de una** fair - haired girl who had pined away **en** the shores **del** Atlantic. Whatever the reason, Ferrier remained strictly celibate. **En** every **otro** respect **él** conformed **a** the religion **del** young settlement, **y** gained the name **de ser** an orthodox **y** straight -

walking man.

Lucy Ferrier grew up within the log - house, **y** assisted **su** adopted father **en todo sus** undertakings. The keen air **de** the mountains **y** the balsamic odour **de los** pine trees took the place **de** nurse **y** mother **a la** young girl. As year succeeded **a** year she grew taller **y** stronger, **ella** cheek more rudy, **y ella** step more elastic. Many a wayfarer upon the high road which ran **por** Ferrier's farm felt long - forgotten thoughts revive **en su** mind as **ellos** watched **a ella** lithe girlish figure tripping through the wheatfields, **o** met **ella** mounted upon **su** father's mustang, **y** managing **eso con toda** the ease **y** grace **de un** true child **del** West. So the bud blossomed into a flower, **y** the year which saw **su** father the richest **de** the farmers left **a ella** as fair a specimen **de** American girlhood as could be found **en** the whole Pacific slope.

No era the father, **sin embargo**, who **primero** discovered that the child had developed into the woman. **Eso** seldom is **en** such cases. That mysterious change is <u>**también**</u> subtle **y también** gradual to be measured **por** dates. Least **de todo** does the maiden herself <u>**saber**</u> **eso** until the tone **de** a voice **o** the touch **de** a hand sets **su** heart thrilling within **ella, y** she learns, **con** a mixture **de** pride **y de** fear, that a **nuevo y** a larger nature has awoken within **ella. Hay** few who can not recall that day **y** remember the one little incident which heralded the dawn **de un nueva vida. En** the case **de** Lucy Ferrier the occasion **era** serious enough **en** itself, apart **de su** future influence **sobre su** destiny **y** that **de** many besides.

Era a warm June morning, **y** the Latter Day Saints **fueron** as busy as the bees whose hive **ellos** have chosen for **su** emblem. **En** the fields **y en** the streets rose the <u>**mismo**</u> hum **de** human industry. Down the dusty high roads defiled long streams **de** heavily - laden mules, **todos** heading **hacia** the west, for the gold fever had broken out **en** California, **y** the Overland Route lay through the City **del** Elect. There, **también**, were droves **de** sheep **y** bullocks coming in **desde el** outlying pasture lands, **y** trains **de** tired immigrants, men **y caballos** equally weary **de su** interminable journey. Through **toda** this motley assemblage, threading **su** way **con** the skill **de un** accomplished rider, there galloped Lucy Ferrier, **su** fair face flushed **con** the exercise **y su** long chestnut hair floating **fuera** behind **ella**. She <u>**tenía**</u> a commission **de su** father **en** the City, **y** was dashing in as she had done many a time **antes, con toda** the fearlessness **de** youth, thinking only **de su** task **y** how **era** to be performed. The travel - stained adventurers gazed **después de** her **en** astonishment, **y incluso** the unemotional Indians, journeying in **con sus** pelties, relaxed **su** accustomed stoicism as **ellos** marvelled at the beauty **de la** pale - faced maiden.

She had reached the outskirts **de** the city when she found the road blocked **por un** great drove **de** cattle, driven **por un** half - dozen wild - looking herdsmen **de** the plains. **En su** impatience she endeavoured to pass this obstacle **por** pushing **su** horse into what appeared to be a gap. Scarcely had she got fairly into **eso, sin embargo, antes de** the beasts closed in behind **ella, y** she found herself completely imbedded **en** the moving stream **de** fierce - eyed, long - horned bullocks. Accustomed as she **era** to deal **con** cattle, she **no estaba** alarmed at **su** situation, **pero** took advantage **de** every opportunity to urge **su** horse on **en** the hopes **de** pushing **su** way through the cavalcade. Unfortunately the horns **de uno de** the creatures, either **por** accident **o** design, came **en** violent contact **con** the flank **de** the mustang, **y** excited it **hacia** madness. **En un instante eso** reared up upon **sus** hind legs **con** a snort **de** rage, **y** pranced **y** tossed **en** a way **eso** would have unseated any **pero** a most skilful rider. The situation **estaba** full **de** peril. Every plunge **del** excited horse brought **eso** against the horns again, **y** goaded **eso hacia** fresh madness. **Era todo** that the girl could **hacer** to keep herself **en** the saddle, yet a slip would mean a terrible death under the hoofs **de los** unwieldy **y** terrified animals. Unaccustomed **a** sudden emergencies, **ella** head began to swim, **y ella** grip upon the bridle to relax. Choked **por el** rising cloud **de** dust **y por** the steam **de las** struggling creatures, she **podría** have abandoned **sus** efforts **en** despair, **pero** for a kindly voice at **ella** elbow which assured **ella de** assistance. At the **mismo** moment a sinewy brown hand caught the frightened horse **por** the curb, **y** forcing a way through the drove, soon brought **a ella hacia** the outskirts.

"**Tú estás** not hurt, **yo** hope, miss," said **su** preserver, respectfully.

She looked up at **su** dark, fierce face, **y** laughed saucily. "**Yo** am awful frightened," she said, naively; "whoever would have thought that Poncho would have been **tan** scared **por** a lot **de** cows?"

"Thank God **tú** kept your seat," the **otro** said earnestly. **Él era** a tall, savage - looking young **tipo**, mounted **en un** powerful roan horse, **y** clad **en** the rough dress **de un cazador, con un** long rifle slung **sobre sus** shoulders. "**Yo** guess **tú eres** the daughter **de** John Ferrier," **él** remarked, "**yo** saw **a ti** ride down **de su** house. When **tú** see him, ask him **si él** remembers the Jefferson Hopes **de** St. Louis. **Si él** is the **mismo** Ferrier, my father **y él** were pretty thick."

"Hadn't **tú** better come **y** ask yourself?" she asked, demurely.

The young **tipo** seemed pleased at the suggestion, **y sus** dark eyes sparkled **con** pleasure. "**Yo** will **hacer** so," **él** said, "**nosotros** have been **en** the mountains for two months, **y** are not over **y** above **en** visiting condition. **Él** must **llevar** us as **él** finds us."

"**Él tiene** a **bien** deal to thank **a ti** for, **y** so **tengo yo**," she answered, "**él tiene** awful fond **de mí. Si aquellas** cows had jumped **en** me **él** would have never got **sobre** it."

"Neither would **yo**," said **su compañera**.

" **Tú!** Well, **yo** don't see that **eso** would make much matter **a ti**, anyhow. **Tú** ain't even a friend **de** ours."

The young hunter's dark face grew **tan** gloomy **sobre** this remark that Lucy Ferrier laughed aloud.

"There, **yo** did not mean that," she said; "**por supuesto, tú eres** a friend now. **Tú** must come **y** see us. Now **yo** must push along, **o** father won't trust me **con su** business **nunca más**. **Adiós!**"

"**Adiós**," **él** answered, raising **su** broad sombrero, **y** bending **sobre su** little hand. She wheeled **su** mustang round, gave **eso** a cut **con su** riding - whip, **y** darted away down the broad road **en** a rolling cloud **de** dust.

Young Jefferson Hope rode on **con sus** companions, gloomy **y** taciturn. **Él y ellos** had been among the Nevada Mountains prospecting for silver, **y** were returning **a** Salt Lake City **en** the hope **de** raising capital enough to **trabajar** some lodes which **ellos** had discovered. **Él** had been as keen as **cualquiera de ellos** upon the business until this sudden incident had drawn **sus** thoughts into **otro** channel. **La vista de la** fair young girl, as frank **y** wholesome as the Sierra breezes, had stirred **su** volcanic, untamed heart **a sus** very depths. When she had vanished **de su vista, él** realized that a crisis had come **en su vida, y** that neither silver speculations nor **ninguna otras** questions could ever be **de** such importance **para** him as this **nuevo y** all - absorbing one. The love which had sprung up **en su** heart **no estaba** the sudden, changeable fancy **de** a boy, **pero** rather the wild, fierce passion **de** a man **de** strong will **y** imperious temper. **Él** had been accustomed to succeed **en todo** that **él** undertook. **Él** swore en **su** heart that **él** would not fail **en** this **si** human effort **y** human perseverance could render him successful.

Él called on John Ferrier that night, **y** many times again, until **su** face **era** a familiar **una** at the farm - house. John, cooped up **en** the valley, **y** absorbed **en su trabajo, había tenido** little chance **de** learning the news **del** outside **mundo** during the last twelve years. **Todo** this Jefferson Hope **era** able to tell him, **y en** a style which interested Lucy as well as **su** father. **Él** had been a pioneer **en** California, **y** could narrate many a strange tale **de** fortunes made **y** fortunes lost **en aquellos** wild, halcyon days. **Él** had been a scout **también, y** a trapper, a silver explorer, **y** a ranchman. Wherever stirring adventures were to be had, Jefferson Hope had been there **en** search **de ellos. Él** soon became a favourite **con el** old farmer, who spoke eloquently **de sus** virtues. **En** such occasions, Lucy **era** silent, **pero su** blushing cheek **y sus** bright, happy eyes, showed only **también** clearly that **su** young heart **era** no longer her own. **Su** honest father may not have observed these symptoms, **pero ellos eran** assuredly not thrown away upon the man who had won **sus** affections.

Era a summer evening when **él** came galloping down the road **y** pulled up at the gate. She **era** at the doorway, **y** came down to meet him. **Él** threw the bridle **sobre** the fence **y** strode up the pathway.

"**Yo** am off, Lucy," **él** said, taking **sus** two **manos en** his, **y** gazing tenderly down into **su** face; "**yo** won't ask **a ti** to come <u>**conmigo**</u> now, **pero** will **tú** be ready to come when **yo** am here again?"

"**Y** when will **eso** be?" she asked, blushing **y** laughing.

"A couple **de** months at the outside. **Yo** will come **y** claim **a ti entonces**, my darling. There is **nadie** who can stand **entre** us."

"**Y** how about father?" she asked.

"**Él** has given **su** consent, provided **nosotros** get these mines working all right. **Yo tengo** no fear **en** that head."

"Oh, well; **por supuesto, si tú y** father have arranged **eso** all, **no hay** more to be said," she whispered, **con su** cheek against **su** broad breast.

"Thank God!" **Él** said, hoarsely, stooping **y** kissing **a ella**. "**Eso** is settled, **entonces**. The longer **yo** stay, the harder **eso** will be to **ir**. **Ellos** are waiting for me at the cañon. **Adiós**, my own darling -- **adiós**. **En** two months **tú** shall see me."

Él tore himself **de ella** as **él** spoke, **y**, flinging himself upon **su** horse, galloped furiously away, never **incluso** looking round, as though afraid that **su** resolution **podría** fail him **si él** took **uno** glance at what **él** was leaving. She stood at the gate, gazing **después** him until **él** vanished **de su vista**. <u>**Luego**</u> she walked back into the house, the happiest girl **en todo** Utah.

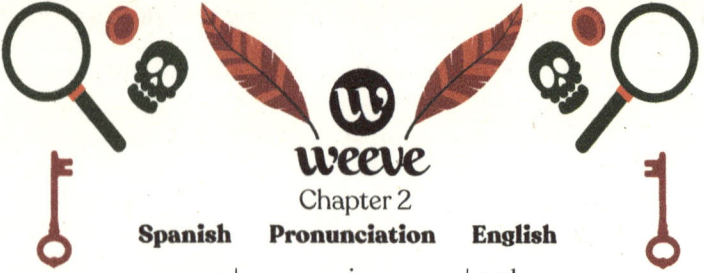

Chapter 2

Spanish	Pronunciation	English
y	i	and
cazador	kasadoɾ	hunter
nuevos	nwebos	new
cualquiera	kwalkjeɾa	any
también	tambjen	too
saber	sabeɾ	know
mismo	mismo	same
tenía	tenja	had
adiós	adjos	good
conmigo	konmigo	with me
luego	lwego	then

3

JOHN FERRIER TALKS WITH THE PROPHET

Weeve Reading Tip: When using our vocab tables to check your knowledge, remember that these show what the words mean in this specific context. Often, this word could have a different meaning when you see it elsewhere. Continue focusing on understanding the word as you see it in the story. Understanding will come naturally with time.

Three weeks had passed since Jefferson Hope **y su** comrades had departed **de** Salt Lake City. John Ferrier's heart **era** sore within him when **él** thought **de la** young man's return, **y de la** impending loss **de su** adopted child. Yet **su** bright **y** happy face reconciled him to the arrangement **más** than **cualquier** argument could have done. **Él fue** always determined, deep down **en su** resolute heart, that nothing would ever induce him to allow **su** daughter to **nosotros** d a Mormon. **Tal** a marriage **él** regarded as no marriage **para nada, pero** as a shame **y** a disgrace. Whatever **él podría pensar en las** Mormon doctrines, upon that one point **él era** inflexible. **Él** had to seal **su** mouth **en** the subject, **sin embargo,** for to express an unorthodox opinion **era** a dangerous matter **en aquellos** days **en** the Land **de los** Saints.

Yes, a dangerous matter -- **tan** dangerous that **incluso** the **mayoría** saintly dared only whisper **su** religious opinions **con** bated breath, lest something which fell **de sus labios podría** be misconstrued, **y** bring down a swift retribution upon **ellos.** The victims **de** persecution had now turned persecutors **sobre su** own account, **y** persecutors **de la mayoría** terrible description. Not the Inquisition **de** Seville, nor the German Vehm - gericht, nor the Secret Societies **de** Italy, were ever able to put a **más** formidable machinery **en** motion than that which cast a cloud

sobre the State **de** Utah.

Su invisibility, **y el misterio** which **era** attached **a eso**, made this organization doubly terrible. **Eso** appeared to be omniscient **y** omnipotent, **y** yet **era** neither seen nor heard. The man who held out against the Church vanished away, **y** none knew whither **él** had gone **o** what had befallen him. **Su** wife **y su** children awaited him at home, **pero** no father ever returned to tell **ellos** how **él** had fared at **las manos de su** secret judges. A rash word **o** a hasty act **era** followed **por** annihilation, **y** yet none knew what the nature **podía ser de** this terrible power which **era** suspended **sobre ellos**. No wonder **que los hombres** went about **en** fear **y** trembling, **y** that **incluso en** the heart **de** the wilderness **ellos** dared not whisper the doubts which oppressed **ellos**.

Al principio this vague **y** terrible power **era** exercised only upon the recalcitrants who, having embraced the Mormon faith, wished afterwards to pervert **o** to abandon **eso**. Soon, **sin embargo, eso** took a wider range. The supply **de** adult women was running short, **y** polygamy without a female population **en** which to draw **era** a barren doctrine indeed. Strange rumours began to be bandied about -- rumours **de** murdered immigrants **y** rifled camps **en** regions where Indians had never been seen. Fresh women appeared **en** the harems **de los** Elders -- women who pined **y** wept, **y** bore upon **sus** faces the traces **de un** unextinguishable horror. Belated wanderers upon the mountains spoke **de** gangs **de** armed **hombres**, masked, stealthy, **y** noiseless, who flitted **por ellos en** the darkness. These tales **y** rumours took substance **y** shape, **y fueron** corroborated **y** re - corroborated, until **ellos** resolved themselves into a definite name. **Para** this day, **en** the lonely ranches **del** West, the name **de la** Danite Band, **o** the Avenging Angels, is a sinister **y** an ill - omened one.

Fuller knowledge **de** the organization which produced **tal** terrible results served to increase rather than to lessen the horror which **eso** inspired **en** the minds **de hombres**. None knew who belonged **a** this ruthless society. The names **de** the participators **en** the deeds **de** blood **y** violence done under the name **de** religion **fueron** kept profoundly secret. The very friend **a** whom **tú** communicated your misgivings as **al** Prophet **y su** mission, **podía ser uno de esos** who would come forth at night **con** fire **y** sword to exact a terrible reparation. Hence every man feared **su** neighbour, **y** none spoke **de las cosas** which **estaban** nearest **su** heart.

Una fine morning, John Ferrier **era** about to set **fuera a sus** wheatfields, when **él** heard the click **de** the latch, **y**, looking through the window, saw a stout, sandy - haired, middle - aged man coming up the pathway. **Su** heart leapt **a su** mouth, for this **era** none **otro** than the **gran** Brigham Young himself. Full **de** trepidation -- for **él** knew that **tal** a visit boded him little **bien** --

Ferrier ran **hacia** the door to greet the Mormon chief. The latter, **sin embargo**, received **sus** salutations coldly, **y** followed him **con un** stern face into the sitting - room.

"Brother Ferrier," **él** said, taking a seat, **y** eyeing the farmer keenly **de** under **su** light - coloured eyelashes, "the true believers have been **buenos** friends **para ti. Nosotros** picked **a ti** up when **tú** were starving **en** the desert, **nosotros** shared our food **contigo**, led **a ti** safe **al** Chosen Valley, gave **a ti** a goodly share **de** land, **y** allowed **a ti** to wax rich under our protection. Is not this **así**?"

"**Eso** is **así**," answered John Ferrier.

"**En** return for **todo** this **nosotros** asked but **una** condition: **eso era**, that **tú deberías** embrace the true faith, **y** conform **en** every way **a sus** usages. This **tú** promised to **hacer, y** this, **si** common report says truly, **tú** have neglected."

"**Y** how have **yo** neglected **eso**?" asked Ferrier, throwing **fuera sus manos en** expostulation. "Have **yo no** given **al** common fund? Have **yo no** attended at the Temple? Have **yo** not----?"

"Where **están** your wives?" asked Young, looking round him. "Call **ellas** in, that **yo** may greet **ellas**."

"**Eso** is true that **yo** have not married," Ferrier answered. "**Pero** women were few, **y** there **fueron muchos** who **tenía** better claims than **yo. Yo no era** a lonely man: **tuve** my daughter to attend **a** my wants."

"**Eso** is of that daughter that **yo** would speak **a ti**," said the leader **de los** Mormons. "She has grown to be the flower **de** Utah, **y** has found favour **en** the eyes **de muchos** who **están** high **en** the land."

John Ferrier groaned internally.

"**Hay** stories **de ella** which **yo** would fain disbelieve -- stories that she is sealed **a algo** Gentile. This must be the gossip **de** idle tongues. What is the thirteenth rule **en** the code **del** sainted Joseph Smith? 'Letevery maiden **de la** true faith marry **uno de** the elect; for **si** she **nosotros** d a Gentile, she commits a grievous sin.' This being **así, eso** is impossible that **tú**, who profess the holy creed, **deberías** suffer your daughter to violate **eso**."

John Ferrier made no answer, **pero él** played nervously **con su** riding - whip.

"Upon this **uno** point your whole faith shall be tested -- **así que ha sido** decided **en** the Sacred Council **de** Four. The girl is young, **y nosotros** would not have her **nosotros** d grey hairs, neither would **nosotros** deprive **ella de todo** choice. **Nosotros** Elders **tenemos muchos** heifers, **pero** our children must also be provided. Stangerson **tiene** a son, **y** Drebber **tiene** a son, **y** either **de ellos** would gladly welcome your daughter **a su** house. Let **ella** choose **entre ellos. Son** young **y** rich, **y de la** true faith. What say **tú a eso**?"

Ferrier remained silent for some little time **con su** brows knitted.

"**Tú** will give **nosotros** time," **él** said at last. "My daughter is very young -- she is scarce **de** an age to marry."

"She shall **tener** a month to choose," said Young, rising **de su** seat. "At the end **de** that time she shall give **su** answer."

Él was passing through the door, when **él** turned, **con** flushed face **y** flashing eyes. "**Era** better for **ti**, John Ferrier," **él** thundered, "that **tú y** she were now lying blanched skeletons upon the Sierra Blanco, than that **debería** put your weak wills against the orders **del** Holy Four!"

Con un threatening gesture **de su** hand, **él** turned **de** the door, **y** Ferrier heard **su** heavy step scrunching along the shingly path.

Él era still sitting **con sus** elbows upon **sus** knees, considering how **él debería** broach the matter **a su** daughter when a soft hand **estaba** laid upon his, **y** looking up, **él** saw **ella** standing beside him. **Una** glance at **su** pale, frightened face showed him that she had heard what had passed.

"**Yo** could **no ayudar eso**," she said, **en** answer **a su mirada**. "**Su** voice rang through the house. Oh, father, father, what shall **hacemos**?"

"Don't **tú** scare yourself," **él** answered, drawing **ella a** him, **y** passing **su** broad, rough hand caressingly **sobre su** chestnut hair. "**Nosotros** will fix **eso** up somehow **o** another. **No encuentras** your fancy kindo' lessening for this chap, do you?"

A sob **y** a squeeze **de su** hand **era su** only answer.

" **No ; por supuesto que no . Yo** shouldn't care to hear **a ti** say **tú** did. **El tiene** a likely lad, **y él** is a Christian, which is **más** than these folk here, **en** spiteo' **todo su** praying **y** preaching. There is a party starting for Nevada tomorrow, **y yo** will manage to send him a message letting him **saber** the hole **nosotros estamos** in. **Si sé** anythingo' that young man, **él** will be back here **con** a speed **que** would whip electro - telegraphs."

Lucy laughed through **sus** tears at **su** father's description.

"When **él** comes, **él** will advise **nosotros** for the **mejor. Pero eso** is for **ti** that **yo** am frightened, dear. **Uno** hears -- **uno** hears **tal** dreadful stories **sobre aquellos** who oppose the Prophet: something terrible always happens **a ellos**."

"**Pero nosotros** haven't opposed him yet," **su** father answered. "**Eso** will be time to **mirar fuera** for squalls when we do. **Tenemos** a clear month **antes de nosotros**; at the end **de eso, yo** guess **tuvimos mejor** shin **fuera de** Utah."

"Leave Utah!"

"**Eso** is **sobre** the size **de** it."

"**Pero** the farm?"

"**Nosotros** will raise as much as **nosotros** can **en** money, **y** let the rest **ir**. To tell the truth, Lucy, **eso** isn't the **primera** time **yo** have thought **de** doing **eso. Yo** don't care **sobre** knuckling under **a cualquier** man, as these folk **hacen a su** darned prophet. **Yo** am a free - born American, **y eso** is **todo nuevo para** me. Guess **yo** am **también** old to learn. **Si él** comes browsing **sobre** this farm, **él podría** chance to run up against a charge **de** buckshot travelling **en** the opposite direction."

"**Pero ellos** won't let **nosotros** leave," **su** daughter objected.

"Wait till Jefferson comes, **y nosotros** will soon manage that. **En** the meantime, don't **tú** fret yourself, my dearie, **y** don't get your eyes swelled up, else **él** will be walking into me when **él** sees **a ti**. There is nothing to be afeared about, **y no hay** danger **para nada**."

John Ferrier uttered these consoling remarks **en** a very confident tone, **pero** she could **no ayudar** observing that **él** paid unusual care **a** the fastening **de** the doors that night, **y** that **él** carefully cleaned **y** loaded the rusty old shotgun which hung upon the wall **de su** bedroom.

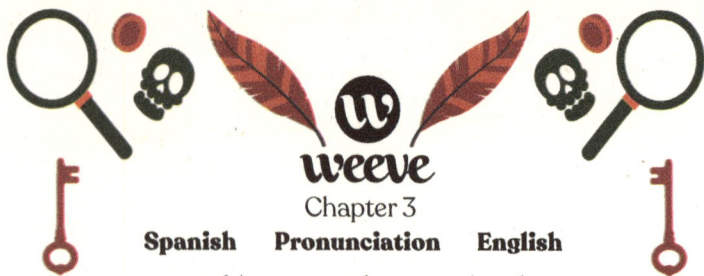

Spanish	Pronunciation	English
tal	tal	such
mayoría	maiorja	most
gran	gran	great
buenos	bwenos	good
ellas	ejas	them
muchos	mutʃos	many
tuve	tube	i had
ha sido	a sido	it has been
hacemos	asemos	we do
sé	se	i know
tuvimos	tubimos	we had
hacen	asen	do

4

A FLIGHT FOR LIFE

En the morning which followed **su** interview **con el** Mormon Prophet, John Ferrier went in **a** Salt Lake City, **y** having found **su** acquaintance, who **era** bound for the Nevada **Montañas**, **él** entrusted him **con su** message **para** Jefferson Hope. **En** it **él** told the young man **del** imminent danger which threatened **ellos**, **y cómo** necessary **era** that **él debería** return. Having done thus **él** felt easier **en su** mind, **y** returned home **con un** lighter heart.

As **él** approached **su** farm, **él era** surprised to see a horse hitched **a cada de** the posts **de** the gate. **Todavía más** surprised **era él** on entering to **encontrar** two young **hombres en** possession **de su** sitting - room. **Uno**, **con un** long pale face, was leaning back **en** the rocking - chair, **con sus pies** cocked up upon the stove. The **otro**, a bull - necked youth **con** coarse bloated features, was standing **en** front **de** the window **con sus manos en su bolsillo**, whistling a popular hymn. Both **de ellos** nodded **hacia** Ferrier as **él** entered, **y** the one **en** the rocking - chair commenced the conversation.

"Quizás no nos conoces" , **dijo** . "This here is the son **de** Elder Drebber, **y yo** am Joseph Stangerson, who travelled **contigo en** the desert when the Lord stretched **fuera Su** hand **y** gathered **a ti** into the true fold."

"As **Él** will **todas** the nations **en Su** own **buen** time," said the

otro en a nasal voice; "**Él** grindeth slowly **pero** exceeding small."

John Ferrier bowed coldly. **Él** had guessed who **su** visitors **eran**.

"**Nosotros** have come," continued Stangerson, "at the advice **de** our fathers to solicit the hand **de** your daughter for whichever **de nosotros** may seem **bien para ti y para ella**. As **yo tengo** but four wives **y** Brother Drebber here **tiene** seven, **eso** appears **a** me that my claim is the stronger one."

"Nay, nay, Brother Stangerson," cried the **otro**; "the question is not <u>**cuantas**</u> wives **tenemos, pero cuantas** <u>**podemos**</u> keep. My father has now given over **sus** mills **a** me, **y yo** am the richer man."

"**Pero** my prospects **están** better," said the **otro**, warmly. "When the Lord removes my father, **yo** shall **tener su** tanning yard **y su** leather factory. Then **yo** am your elder, **y** am higher **en** the Church."

"**Eso** will be for the maiden to decide," rejoined young Drebber, smirking at **su** own reflection **en** the glass. "**Nosotros** will leave **eso todo** to **su** decision."

During this dialogue, John Ferrier had stood fuming **en** the doorway, hardly able to keep **su** riding - whip **de** the backs **de sus** two visitors.

"**Mira** here," **él** said at last, striding up **hacia ellos**, "when my daughter summons **a vosotros, vosotros podeis** come, **pero** until **entonces yo** don't want to see your faces again."

The two young Mormons stared at him **en** amazement. **En sus ojos** this competition **entre ellos** for the maiden's hand **era** the highest **de** honours both **para ella y su** father.

"**Hay** two ways out **de** the room," cried Ferrier; "there is the door, **y** there is the window. Which do **vosotros** care to use?"

Su brown face looked **tan** savage, **y su** gaunt **manos tan** threatening, that **sus** visitors sprang **a sus pies y** beat a hurried retreat. The old farmer followed **ellos hacia** the door.

"Let me **saber** when **vosotros** have settled which it is to be," **él** said, sardonically.

"**Tú** shall smart for this!" Stangerson cried, white **con** rage. "**Tú** have defied the Prophet **y** the Council **de** Four. **Tú** shall rue **eso a** the end **de** your <u>**días**</u>."

"The hand **del** Lord shall be heavy upon **ti**," cried young Drebber; "**Él** will arise **y** smite **ti**!"

"**Entonces yo** will start the smiting," exclaimed Ferrier furiously, y would have rushed upstairs for **su** gun had not Lucy seized him **por** the arm **y** restrained him. **Antes de él** could escape **de ella**, the clatter **de caballos'** hoofs told him that **ellos eran** beyond **su** reach.

"The young canting rascals!" **Él** exclaimed, wiping the perspiration **de su** forehead; "**yo** would sooner see **a ti en** your grave, my girl, than the wife **de** either **de ellos**."

"**Y así debería yo**, father," she answered, **con** spirit; "**pero** Jefferson will soon be here."

"Yes. **Eso** will not be long **antes de él** comes. The sooner the better, for **no sabemos** what **su** next move may be."

Era, indeed, high time that someone capable **de** giving advice **y ayuda debería** come **a** the aid **del** sturdy old farmer **y su** adopted daughter. **En** the whole history **de** the settlement there had never been **tal** a case **de** rank disobedience **a** the authority **de los** Elders. **Si** minor errors **fueron** punished **tan** sternly, what would be the fate **de** this arch rebel. Ferrier knew that **su** wealth **y** position would be **de** no avail **a** him. Others as well known **y** as rich as himself had been spirited away **antes de** now, **y sus** goods given over **a la** Church. **Él era** a brave man, **pero él** trembled at the vague, shadowy terrors which hung **sobre** him. **Cualquier** known danger **él** could face **con un** firm lip, **pero** this suspense **era** unnerving. **Él** concealed **sus** fears **de su** daughter, **sin embargo, y** affected to make light **del** whole matter, though she, **con el** keen eye **de** love, saw plainly that **él era** ill at ease.

Él expected that **él** would receive some message **o** remonstrance **de** Young as to **su** conduct, **y él no estaba** mistaken, though **eso** came **en** an unlooked - for manner. Upon rising next morning **él** found, **para su** surprise, a small square **de** paper pinned on **a** the coverlet **de su** bed **solo sobre su** chest. On **estaba** printed, **en** bold straggling letters: --

"Twenty - nine **días** are given **a ti** for amendment, **y** then----"

The dash **era más** fear - inspiring than **cualquier** threat could have been. **Cómo** this warning came into **su** room puzzled John Ferrier sorely, for **sus** servants slept **en** an outhouse, **y** the doors **y** windows had **todas** been secured. **Él** crumpled the paper up **y** said nothing **a su** daughter, **pero** the incident struck a chill into **su** heart. The twenty - nine **días fueron** evidently the balance **de** the month which Young had promised. What strength **o** courage could avail against an enemy armed **con tal** mysterious powers? The hand which fastened that pin **podría** have struck him **a** the heart, **y él** could never have known who had slain him.

Todavía más shaken **estaba él** next morning. **Ellos** had sat down **a su** breakfast when Lucy **con** a cry **de** surprise pointed upwards.

En the centre **de** the ceiling **estaba** scrawled, **con un** burned stick apparently, the number 28. **Para su** daughter **era** unintelligible, **y él** did not enlighten **ella**. That night **él** sat up **con su** gun **y** kept watch **y** ward. **Él** saw **y él** heard nothing, **y** yet **en** the morning a **gran** 27 had been painted upon the outside **de su** door.

Thus day followed day; **y** as sure as morning came **él** found that **sus** unseen enemies had kept **su** register, **y** had marked up **en** some conspicuous position **cuántos días** were **todavía** left **a** him out **de** the month **de** grace. Sometimes the fatal numbers appeared upon the walls, sometimes upon the floors, occasionally **ellos eran sobre** small placards stuck upon the garden gate **o** the railings. **Con toda su** vigilance John Ferrier could not discover whence these daily warnings proceeded. A horror which **era** almost superstitious came upon him at **la vista de ellos. Él** became haggard **y** restless, **y sus ojos <u>tenían</u>** the troubled **mirada de algún** hunted creature. **Él tuvo** but **una** hope **en vida** now, **y ese era** for the arrival **del** young **cazador de** Nevada.

Twenty had changed **a** fifteen **y** fifteen to ten, **pero no había ninguna** news **de** the absentee. **Uno por uno** the numbers dwindled down, **y todavía** there came no sign **de él.** Whenever a horseman clattered down the road, **o** a driver shouted at **su** team, the old farmer hurried **hacia** the gate thinking **que ayuda** had arrived at last. At last, when **él** saw five give way **a** four **y** that again **a** three, **él** lost heart, **y** abandoned **toda** hope **de** escape. Single - handed, **y con su** limited knowledge **de las montañas** which surrounded the settlement, **él** knew that **él era** powerless. The **más** - frequented roads **fueron** strictly watched **y** guarded, **y** none could pass along **ellos** without an order **de el** Council. Turn which way **él** would, there appeared to be no avoiding the blow which hung **sobre** him. Yet the old man never wavered **en su** resolution to part **con vida** itself **antes de él** consented **a** what **él** regarded as **su** daughter's dishonour.

Él was sitting alone **una** evening pondering deeply **sobre sus** troubles, **y** searching vainly for some way out **de ellos.** That morning had shown the figure 2 upon the wall **de su** house, **y** the next day would be the last **del** allotted time. What **<u>iba</u>** to happen **entonces? Toda** manner **de** vague **y** terrible fancies filled **su** imagination. **Y su** daughter -- what **iba** to become **de ella después él** was gone? Was there no escape **de la** invisible network which **estaba** drawn all round **ellos. Él** sank **su** head upon the table **y** sobbed at the thought **de su** own impotence.

What **era eso? En** the silence **él** heard a gentle scratching sound -- low, **pero** very distinct **en** the quiet **de** the night. **Eso** came **de** the door **de** the house. Ferrier crept into the hall **y** listened intently. **Hubo** a pause for **unos pocos** moments, **y entonces** the low insidious sound **era** repeated. Someone was evidently tapping very gently upon **uno de** the panels **de** the door. Was

eso some midnight assassin who had come to carry out the murderous orders **del** secret tribunal? **O era eso** some agent who was marking up that the last day **de** grace had arrived. John Ferrier felt that instant death would be better than the suspense which shook **sus** nerves **y** chilled **su** heart. Springing forward **él** drew the bolt **y** threw the door open.

Outside **todo estaba** calm **y** quiet. The night **era** fine, **y** the stars were twinkling brightly overhead. The little front garden lay **antes de** the farmer's **ojos** bounded **por** the fence **y** gate, **pero** neither there nor **en** the road **era** any **ser humano** to be seen. **Con** a sigh **de** relief, Ferrier looked **a la derecha y** to left, until happening to glance straight down at **sus** own **pies él** saw **para su** astonishment a man lying flat upon **su** face upon the ground, **con** arms **y** legs **todos** asprawl.

Tan unnerved **era él** at **la vista** that **él** leaned up against the wall **con su** hand **hacia su** throat to stifle **su** inclination to call out. **Su primer** thought **era** that the prostrate figure **era** that **de** some wounded **o** dying man, **pero** as **él** watched **eso él** saw **eso** writhe along the ground **y** into the hall **con** the rapidity **y** noiselessness **de** a serpent. Once within the house the man sprang **a sus pies**, closed the door, **y** revealed **al** astonished farmer the fierce face **y** resolute expression **de** Jefferson Hope.

"Good God!" gasped John Ferrier. "**Cómo tú** scared me! Whatever made **a ti** come in **como** that."

"Give me food," the **otro** said, hoarsely. "**Yo he tenido** no time for bite **o** sup for eight - **y** - forty hours." **Él** flung himself upon the cold meat **y** bread which were **todavía** lying upon the table **de su** host's supper, **y** devoured **eso** voraciously. "Does Lucy bear up well?" **Él** asked, when **él** had satisfied **su** hunger.

"Yes. She **no sabe** the danger," **su** father answered.

"**Eso** is well. The house is watched **en** every side. **Eso** is **por qué yo** crawled my way up **a** it. **Ellos pueden** be darned sharp, **pero ellos no son** quite sharp enough to catch a Washoe **cazador**."

John Ferrier felt a different man now that **él** realized that **él tuvo** a devoted ally. **Él** seized the young man's leathery hand **y** wrung **eso** cordially. "**Tú eres** a man to be proud of," **él** said. "**No hay muchos** who would come to share our danger **y** our troubles."

"**Tú** have hit **eso** there, pard," the young **cazador** answered. "**Yo tengo** a respect for **ti, pero si** <u>estabas</u> alone **en** this business **yo** would **pensar** twice **antes de yo** put my head into **tal** a hornet's nest. It is Lucy that brings mc here, **y antes de** harm comes **sobre ella Yo** guess there will be one lesso' the Hope family **en** Utah."

"Qué vamos a hacer ?"

"Tomorrow is your last day, **y** unless **tú** act tonight **tú estás** lost. **Yo tengo** a mule **y** two **caballos** waiting **en** the Eagle Ravine. **Cuánto dinero tienes ?**"

"Two thousand dollars **en** gold, **y** five **en** notes."

"**Eso** will do. **Yo tengo** as much **más** to add **a eso**. **Nosotros** must push for Carson City through **las montañas**. **Tú** had **mejor** wake Lucy. **Eso** is as well that the servants do not sleep **en** the house."

Mientras Ferrier **estaba** absent, preparing **su** daughter for the approaching journey, Jefferson Hope packed **todos** the eatables that **él** could **encontrar** into a small parcel, **y** filled a stoneware jar **con agua**, for **él** knew **por** experience that the mountain wells **eran pocos y** far between. **Él había** hardly completed **sus** arrangements **antes de** the farmer returned **con su** daughter **toda** dressed **y** ready for a start. The greeting **entre** the lovers **fue** warm, **pero** brief, for minutes **eran** precious, **y había mucho** to be done.

"**Nosotros** must make our start at once," said Jefferson Hope, speaking **en** a low **pero** resolute voice, **como uno** who realizes the greatness **de** the peril, **pero** has steeled **su** heart to meet it. "The front **y** back entrances **están** watched, **pero con** caution **nosotros podríamos** get away through the side window **y** across the fields. Once **en** the road **nosotros estamos** only two miles **del** Ravine where **los caballos** are waiting. **Por** daybreak **deberíamos** be half - way through **las montañas**."

"What **si nosotros somos** stopped," asked Ferrier.

Hope slapped the revolver butt which protruded **de** the front **de su** tunic. "**Si ellos son también muchos** for **nosotros nosotros** shall **llevar** two **o** three **de ellos con nosotros**," **él** said **con una** sinister smile.

The lights inside the house had **todas** been extinguished, **y desde la** darkened window Ferrier peered **sobre** the fields which had been his own, **y** which **él era** now about to abandon for ever. **Él tuvo** long nerved himself **a** the sacrifice, **sin embargo**, **y** the thought **de** the honour **y** happiness **de su** daughter outweighed **cualquier** regret at **sus** ruined fortunes. **Todo** looked **tan** peaceful **y** happy, the rustling trees **y** the broad silent stretch **de** grain - land, that **era** difficult to realize that the spirit **de asesinato** lurked through **eso** all. Yet the white face **y** set expression **del** young **cazador** showed that **en su** approach **a** the house **él** had seen enough to satisfy him upon that head.

Ferrier carried the bag **de** gold **y** notes, Jefferson Hope **tenía** the scanty provisions **y agua**, **mientras** Lucy **tenía** a small bundle containing **unos pocos de sus más** valued possessions. Opening the window very slowly **y** carefully, **ellos** waited until a dark cloud had somewhat obscured the night, **y entonces uno por uno** passed through into the little garden. **Con** bated breath **y** crouching figures **ellos** stumbled across **eso, y** gained the shelter **de** the hedge, which **ellos** skirted until **ellos** came **hacia** the gap which opened into the cornfields. **Ellos habían justo** reached this point when the young man seized **sus** two companions **y** dragged **ellos** down into the shadow, where **ellos** lay silent **y** trembling.

Era as well that su prairie training had given Jefferson Hope the ears **de** a lynx. **Él y sus** friends had hardly crouched down **antes de** the melancholy hooting **de** a mountain owl **fue** heard within **unos pocos** yards **de ellos**, which **fue** immediately answered **por otra** hoot at a small distance. At the **mismo** moment a vague shadowy figure emerged **desde** the gap for which **ellos habían** been making, **y** uttered the plaintive signal cry again, **en** which a second man appeared **fuera de** the obscurity.

"Tomorrow at midnight," said the **primero** who appeared to be **en** authority. "When the Whip - poor - will calls three times."

"**Eso** is well," returned the **otro**. "Shall **yo** tell Brother Drebber?"

"Pass **eso** on **a** him, **y de** him **a** the others. Nine **a** seven!"

"Seven to five!" repeated the **otro, y** the two figures flitted away **en** different directions. **Su** concluding **palabras** had evidently been some form **de** sign **y** countersign. **El instante** that **sus** footsteps had died away **en** the distance, Jefferson Hope sprang **hacia sus pies, y** helping **sus** companions through the gap, led the way across the fields at the top **de su** speed, supporting **y** half - carrying the girl when **su** strength appeared to fail **le**.

"**Date prisa**! **Date prisa**!" **Él** gasped **de vez en cuando**. "**Nosotros estamos** through the line **de** sentinels. Everything depends **en** speed. **Date prisa**!"

Once **en la** high road **ellos** made rapid progress. Only once did **ellos** meet anyone, **y entonces ellos** managed to slip into a field, **y así** avoid recognition. **Antes de** reaching the town **el cazador** branched away into a rugged **y** narrow footpath which led **a las montañas**. Two dark jagged peaks loomed above **ellos** through the darkness, **y** the defile which led **entre ellos era** the Eagle Cañon **en** which **los caballos** were awaiting **ellos. Con** unerring instinct Jefferson Hope picked **su** way among the **grandes** boulders **y** along the bed **de un** dried - up watercourse, until **él** came **al** retired corner, screened **con** rocks, where the faithful animals had been picketed. The girl **fue** placed upon the mule, **y** old Ferrier upon **uno de los caballos, con su** money - bag, **mientras** Jefferson Hope led the **otro** along the precipitous **y** dangerous path.

Era a bewildering route for anyone who **no estuviera** accustomed to face Nature **en su** wildest moods. **En** the **un** side a **gran** crag towered up a thousand **pies o más**, black, stern, **y** menacing, **con** long basaltic columns upon **su** rugged surface **como** the ribs **de algunos** petrified monster. **En la otra** hand a wild chaos **de** boulders **y** debris made **todo** advance impossible. **Entre** the two ran the irregular track, **tan** narrow **en** places that **ellos tenían** to travel **en** Indian file, **y tan** rough **que** only practised riders could have traversed **eso** at all. Yet **en** spite **de todo** dangers **y** difficulties, the hearts **de** the fugitives **fueron** light within **ellos**, for every step increased the distance **entre ellos y** the terrible despotism **de** which **ellos** were flying.

Ellos soon **tenían** a proof, **sin embargo**, that **ellos estaban todavía** within the jurisdiction **de los** Saints. **Ellos** had reached the very wildest **y** <u>**mayor**</u> desolate portion **de** the pass when the girl gave a startled cry, **y** pointed upwards. **Sobre** a rock which overlooked the track, showing out dark **y** plain against the sky, there stood a solitary sentinel. **Él** saw **ellos** as soon as **ellos** perceived him, **y su** military challenge **de** "Who goes there?" rang through the silent ravine.

"Travellers for Nevada," said Jefferson Hope, **con su** hand upon the rifle which hung **por su** saddle.

Ellos could see the lonely watcher fingering **su** gun, **y** peering down at **ellos** as **si** dissatisfied at **su** reply.

"**Por** whose permission?" **Él** asked.

"The Holy Four," answered Ferrier. **Sus** Mormon experiences had taught him that **que era** the highest authority to which **él** could refer.

"Nine **de** seven," cried the sentinel.

"Seven **de** five," returned Jefferson Hope promptly, remembering the countersign which **él** had heard **en** the garden.

"Pass, **y** the Lord **ir contigo**," said the voice **de** above. Beyond **su** post the path broadened out, **y los caballos fueron** able to break into a trot. Looking back, **ellos** could see the solitary watcher leaning upon **su** gun, **y** knew that **ellos** had passed the outlying post **de la** chosen **gente**, **y** that freedom lay **delante de ellos**.

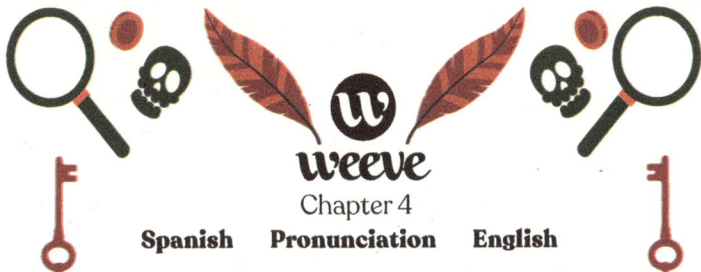

Chapter 4

Spanish	Pronunciation	English
montañas	montaɲas	mountains
cómo	komo	how
todavía	todabja	still
todas	todas	all
buen	bwen	good
cuantas	kwantas	how many
podemos	podemos	we can
días	djas	days
tenían	tenjan	had
iba	iba	was
estabas	estabas	you were
deberíamos	deberjamos	we should
le	le	her
date prisa	date prisa	hurry on
grandes	grandes	great
mayor	maior	most

5

THE AVENGING ANGELS

> "Language acquisition does not require extensive use of conscious grammatical rules, and does not require tedious drill." – Stephen Krashen, expert in linguistics at University of Southern California

Toda night **su** course lay **a través de** intricate defiles **y sobre** irregular **y** rock - strewn paths. **Más que** once **ellos** lost **su** way, **pero** Hope's intimate knowledge **de las montañas** enabled **ellos** to regain the track once **más**. When morning broke, a scene **de** marvellous though savage beauty lay **antes de ellos**. **En** every direction the **gran** snow - capped peaks hemmed **ellos en**, peeping **sobre cada** other's shoulders **al** far horizon. So steep **fueron** the rocky banks **en** either side **de ellos**, that the larch **y** the pine seemed to be suspended **sobre sus** heads, **y** to need **solamente** a gust **de** wind to come hurtling down upon **ellos**. Nor **era** the fear entirely an illusion, for the barren valley **era** thickly strewn **con** trees **y** boulders which had fallen **en** a similar manner. **Incluso** as **ellos** passed, a **gran** rock came thundering down **con un** hoarse rattle which woke the echoes **en** the silent gorges, **y** startled the weary **caballos** into a gallop.

As the sun rose slowly above the eastern horizon, the caps **de las grandes montañas** lit up **uno después de** the **otro, como** lamps at a festival, until **ellos eran todos** ruddy **y** glowing. The magnificent spectacle cheered the hearts **de los** three fugitives **y** gave **ellos** fresh energy. At a wild torrent which swept out **de** a ravine **ellos** called a halt **y** watered **sus caballos, mientras ellos** partook **de un** hasty breakfast. Lucy **y su** father would fain have rested longer, **pero** Jefferson Hope **era** inexorable. "**Ellos** will be
100

upon our track **por** this time," **él** said. "Everything depends upon our speed. Once safe **en** Carson **nosotros podríamos** rest for the remainder **de** our lives."

During the whole **de** that day **ellos** struggled on **a través de** the defiles, **y por** evening **ellos** calculated that **ellos eran más que** thirty miles **de sus** enemies. At night - time **ellos** chose the base **de un** beetling crag, **dónde** the rocks offered some protection **de** the chill wind, **y** there huddled together for warmth, **ellos** enjoyed **unas pocas** hours' sleep. **Antes de** daybreak, **sin embargo, ellos estaban** up **y en su** way once **más. Ellos** had seen no signs **de cualquier** pursuers, **y** Jefferson Hope began to **pensar** that **ellos eran** fairly **fuera de** the reach **de la** terrible organization whose enmity **ellos** had incurred. **Él** little knew **cómo** far that iron grasp could reach, **o cómo** soon **era** to close upon <u>les</u> **y** crush **les.**

Sobre the middle **del** second day **de su** flight **su** scanty store **de** provisions began to <u>acabarse</u>. This gave **el cazador** little uneasiness, **sin embargo,** for **había** game to be had among **las montañas, y él tuvo** frequently **antes de** had to depend upon **su** rifle for the needs **de vida.** Choosing a sheltered nook, **él** piled together **unos pocos** dried branches **y** made a blazing fire, at which **sus** companions **podrían** warm themselves, for **ellos estaban** now nearly five thousand **pies** above the sea level, **y** the air **era** bitter **y** keen. Having tethered **los caballos, y** bade Lucy adieu, **él** threw **su** gun **sobre su** shoulder, **y** set **fuera en** search **de** whatever chance **podría** throw **en su** way. Looking back **él** saw the old man **y** the young girl crouching **sobre** the blazing fire, **mientras** the three animals stood motionless **en** the back - ground. **Entonces** the intervening rocks hid **les de su** view.

Él walked for a couple **de** miles **a través de un** ravine **después de otro** without success, though **desde** the marks upon the bark **de** the trees, **y otras** indications, **él** judged that **habían** numerous bears **en** the vicinity. At last, **después de <u>dos</u> o** three hours' fruitless search, **él** was thinking **de** turning back **en** despair, when casting **sus ojos** upwards **él** saw **una vista** which sent a thrill **de** pleasure **a través de su** heart. **En** the edge **de un** jutting pinnacle, three **o** four hundred **pies** above him, there stood a creature somewhat resembling a sheep **en** appearance, **pero** armed **con** a pair **de** gigantic horns. The big - horn -- for **así eso** is called -- was acting, probably, as a guardian **sobre** a flock which were invisible **al cazador; pero** fortunately **eso** was heading **en** the opposite direction, **y** had not perceived him. Lying **en su** face, **él** rested **su** rifle upon a rock, **y** took a long **y** steady aim **antes de** drawing the trigger. The animal sprang into the air, tottered for a moment upon the edge **de** the precipice, **y entonces** came crashing down into the valley beneath.

The creature **era también** unwieldy to lift, **así que el cazador** contented himself **con** cutting away **uno** haunch **y** part **de** the flank. **Con** this trophy sobre su shoulder, **él** hastened to retrace **sus pasos**, for the evening was already drawing **en**. **Él tuvo** hardly started, **sin embargo, antes de él** realized the difficulty which faced him. **En su** eagerness **él** had wandered far past the ravines which were known **para** him, **y era** no easy matter to pick out the path which **él** had taken. The valley **en** which **él** found himself divided **y** sub - divided into **muchos** gorges, which **fueron** so **como cada otro** that **era** impossible to distinguish **uno del otro**. **Él** followed **uno** for a mile **o más** until **él** came **a** a mountain torrent which **él era** sure that **él** had never seen **antes**. Convinced that **él** had taken the wrong turn, **él** tried **otro, pero con el mismo** result. Night was coming on rapidly, **y era** almost dark **antes de él** at last found himself **en** a defile which **era** familiar **para** him. **Incluso entonces era** no easy matter to keep **a la <u>correcta</u>** track, for the moon **no ha** yet risen, **y** the high cliffs **en** either side made the obscurity **más** profound. Weighed down **con su** burden, **y** weary **de sus** exertions, **él** stumbled along, keeping up **su** heart **por** the reflection that every step brought him nearer **a** Lucy, **y** that **él** carried **con él** enough to ensure **les** food for the remainder **de su** journey.

Él había now come **a** the mouth **del** very defile **en** which **él** had left **les**. **Incluso en** the darkness **él** could recognize the outline **de** the cliffs which bounded it. **Ellos deben, él** reflected, be awaiting him anxiously, for **él** had been absent nearly five hours. **En** the gladness **de su** heart **él** put **sus manos** to **su** mouth **y** made the glen re - echo **a un** loud halloo as a signal that **él** was coming. **Él** paused **y** listened for an answer. None came save **su <u>propio</u>** cry, which clattered up the dreary silent ravines, **y era** borne back **hacia sus** ears **en** countless repetitions. Again **él** shouted, **incluso** louder **que antes, y** again no whisper came back **de** the friends whom **él** had left **tal** a short time ago. A vague, nameless dread came **sobre** him, **y él** hurried onwards frantically, dropping the precious food **en su** agitation.

When **él** turned the corner, **él** came full **a la vista de** the spot **dónde** the fire had been lit. **Había todavía** a glowing pile **de** wood ashes there, **pero** it had evidently not been tended since **su** departure. The **mismo** dead silence **todavía** reigned all round. **Con sus** fears **todos** changed **a** convictions, **él se dio prisa. No había** living creature near the remains **de** the fire: animals, man, maiden, **todos estaban** gone. **Era solamente también** clear that some sudden **y** terrible disaster had occurred during **su** absence -- a disaster which had embraced **a ellos todos, y** yet had left no traces behind **eso**.

Bewildered **y** stunned **por** this blow, Jefferson Hope felt **su** head spin round, **y tenía** to lean upon **su** rifle to save himself **de** falling. **Él era** essentially a man **de** action, **sin embargo, y** speedily recovered **de su** temporary impotence. Seizing a half - consumed piece **de** wood **desde el** smouldering fire, **él** blew eso into a flame, y proceeded con su ayuda to examine the little camp. The ground estaba todo stamped down por los pies de caballos, showing that a large party de mounted hombres had overtaken the fugitives, y the direction de sus tracks proved that ellos tuvieron afterwards turned back para Salt Lake City. Had ellos carried back both de sus companions con ellos? Jefferson Hope had almost persuaded himself that ellos deberían have done así, when su eye fell upon an object which made every nerve de su body tingle within him. A little way en un side de the camp era a low - lying heap de reddish soil, which had assuredly not been there antes. No había mistaking eso for anything pero a newly - dug grave. As the young cazador approached eso, él perceived that a stick had been planted en eso, con a sheet de paper stuck en the cleft fork de eso. The inscription upon the paper era brief, pero to the point:

John Ferrier, Formerly De Salt Lake City, Died August 4th, 1860.

The sturdy old man, whom él had left tan short a time antes, was gone, entonces, y this era todo su epitaph. Jefferson Hope looked wildly round to ver si había a second grave, pero there was no sign de una. Lucy had been carried back por sus terrible pursuers to fulfil su original destiny, por becoming una de the harem del Elder's son. As the young compañero realized the certainty de su fate, y su propio powerlessness to prevent eso, él wished that él, también, was lying con el old farmer en su last silent resting - place.

Again, sin embargo, su active spirit shook off the lethargy which springs de despair. Si había nothing else left para him, él could at least devote su vida to revenge. Con indomitable patience y perseverance, Jefferson Hope possessed also a power de sustained vindictiveness, which él may have learned de los Indians amongst whom él had lived. As él stood por el desolate fire, él felt that the única cosa which could assuage su grief would be thorough y complete retribution, brought por su propio hand upon sus enemies. Su strong will y untiring energy deberían, él determined, be devoted a ese one end. Con una grim, white face, él retraced sus pasos hacia donde él had dropped the food, y having stirred up the smouldering fire, él cooked enough to last him for unos pocos días. This él made up into a bundle, y, tired as él era, él set himself to walk back a través de las montañas upon the track de los avenging angels.

For five días él toiled footsore y weary a través de the defiles which él había already traversed en horseback. At night él flung himself down among the rocks, y snatched unas pocas hours de sleep; pero antes de daybreak él era always bien en su way. En el sixth day, él reached the Eagle Cañon, de which ellos had commenced su ill - fated flight. Thence él could mirWme de the saints. Worn y exhausted, él leaned upon su rifle y shook su gaunt hand fiercely at the silent widespread city beneath him. As **él** looked at **eso**, **él** observed that **habían** flags **en** some **de las** principal streets, **y** **otros** signs **de** festivity. **Él era todavía** speculating as to what this **podría** mean when **él** heard the clatter **de** horse's hoofs, **y** saw a mounted man riding towards him. As **él** approached, **él** recognized him as a Mormon named Cowper, to whom **él** had rendered services at different times. **Él** therefore accosted him when **él** got up **hacia** him, **con** the object **de** finding out what Lucy Ferrier's fate had been.

"**Yo** am Jefferson Hope," **él** said. "**Tú** remember me."

The Mormon looked at him **con** undisguised astonishment -- indeed, **era** difficult to recognize **en** this tattered, unkempt wanderer, **con** ghastly white face **y** fierce, wild **ojos**, the spruce young **cazador de** former **días**. Having, **sin embargo**, at last, satisfied himself as to **su** identity, the man's surprise changed **a** consternation.

"**Tú estás** mad to come here," **él** cried. "**Eso** is as much as my **propia vida** is worth to be seen talking **contigo**. There is a warrant against **ti desde el** Holy Four for assisting the Ferriers away."

"**Yo** don't fear **a ellos**, **o su** warrant," Hope said, earnestly. "**Debes saber** something **de** this matter, Cowper. **Yo** conjure **a ti por** everything **tú** hold dear to answer **unas pocas** questions. **Nosotros tenemos** always been friends. For God's sake, don't refuse to answer me."

"What is **eso**?" the Mormon asked uneasily. "Be quick. The very rocks **tienen** ears **y** the trees **ojos**."

"What has become **de** Lucy Ferrier?"

"She was married yesterday to young Drebber. Hold up, man, hold up, **tú tienes** no **vida** left **en ti**."

"Don't mind me," said Hope faintly. **Él era** white to the very **labios**, **y** had sunk down **sobre** the stone against which **él había** been leaning. "Married, **tú** say?"

"Married yesterday -- **eso** is what **aquellas** flags are for **sobre la** Endowment House. **Había algunas palabras entre** young Drebber **y** young Stangerson as to which was to **tener** her. **Ellos habían** both been **en** the party **que** followed **a ellos**, **y** Stangerson had shot **su** father, which seemed to give him the **mejor** claim; **pero** when **ellos** argued **eso fuera en** council, Drebber's party **era** the stronger, **así que** the Prophet gave **ella** over to him. **Nadie** won't **tener la** very long though, for **yo** saw death **en su** face yesterday. She is **más como** a ghost **que** a woman. Are **tú** off, **entonces**?"

"Yes, **yo** am off," said Jefferson Hope, who had risen **de su** seat. **Su** face **podría haber** been chiselled out **de** marble, **tan** hard **y** set **era su** expression, **mientras sus ojos** glowed **con una** baleful light.

"**A dónde** are **tú** going?"

"Never mind," **él** answered; **y,** slinging **su** weapon **sobre su** shoulder, strode off down the gorge **y tan** away into the heart **de las montañas a** the haunts **de las** wild beasts. Amongst **ellos todos** there was none **tan** fierce **y tan** dangerous as himself.

The prediction **del** Mormon **era solamente también bien** fulfilled. Whether it was the terrible death **de su** father **o** the effects **del** hateful marriage into which she had been forced, poor Lucy never held up **su** head again, **pero** pined away **y** died within a month. **Su** sottish husband, who had married her principally for the sake **de** John Ferrier's property, did not affect any **gran** grief at **su** bereavement; **pero su otras** wives mourned **sobre ella, y** sat up **con ella** the night **antes de** the burial, as is the Mormon custom. **Ellas estaban** grouped round the bier **en** the early hours **de** the morning, when, **para su** inexpressible fear **y** astonishment, the door **era** flung open, **y** a savage - looking, weather - beaten man **en** tattered garments strode into the room. Without a glance **o** a word **a las** cowering women, **él** walked up **hacia la** white silent figure which had once contained the pure soul **de** Lucy Ferrier. Stooping **sobre ella, él** pressed **sus labios** reverently **hacia su** cold forehead, **y entonces,** snatching up **su** hand, **él** took the wedding - ring **de su** finger. "She shall not be buried **en** that," **él** cried **con un** fierce snarl, **y antes de** an alarm could be raised sprang down the stairs **y era** gone. **Tan** strange **y tan** brief **fue** the episode, that the watchers **podrían** have found **eso** hard to believe it themselves **o** persuade **otra gente de eso,** had it not been for the undeniable fact that the circlet **de** gold which marked **a ella** as having been a bride had disappeared.

For some months Jefferson Hope lingered among **las montañas,** leading a strange wild **vida, y** nursing **en su** heart the fierce desire for vengeance which possessed him. Tales **fueron** told **en** the City **del** weird figure which **fue** seen prowling **sobre** the suburbs, **y** which haunted the lonely mountain gorges. Once a bullet whistled **a través de** Stangerson's window **y** flattened itself upon the wall within a foot **de él. En otra** occasion, as Drebber passed under a cliff a **gran** boulder crashed down **sobre** him, **y él solamente** escaped a terrible death **por** throwing himself upon **su** face. The **dos** young Mormons **fueron** not long **en** discovering the reason **de** these attempts upon **sus** lives, **y** led repeated expeditions into **las montañas en** the hope **de** capturing **o** killing **su** enemy, **pero** always without success. **Entonces ellos** adopted the precaution **de** never going **fuera** alone **o después de** nightfall, **y de** having **sus** houses guarded. **Después de** a time

ellos eran able to relax these measures, for nothing **era** either heard **o** seen **de su** opponent, **y ellos** hoped that time had cooled **su** vindictiveness.

Far **de** doing **así**, it had, **si** anything, augmented **eso. La** hunter's mind **era de un** hard, unyielding nature, **y** the predominant idea **de** revenge had taken **tal** complete possession **de** it that **no había** room for **ninguna otra** emotion. **Él era, sin embargo**, above **todas las cosas** practical. **Él** soon realized that **incluso su** iron constitution could not stand the incessant strain which **él** was putting upon it. Exposure **y** want **de** wholesome food were wearing him **fuera. Si él** died **como** a dog among **las montañas**, what **era** to become **de su** revenge **entonces? Y** yet **tal** a death was sure to overtake him **si él** persisted. **Él** felt that **eso era** to play **su** enemy's game, **así que él** reluctantly returned **a las** old Nevada mines, there to recruit **su** health **y** to amass money enough to allow him to pursue **su** object without privation.

Su intention had been to be absent a year at the most, **pero** a combination **de** unforeseen circumstances prevented **su** leaving the mines for nearly five. At the end **de** that time, **sin embargo, su** memory **de su** wrongs **y su** craving for revenge **fueron** quite as keen as **en esa** memorable night when **él** had stood **por** John Ferrier's grave. Disguised, **y** under an assumed name, **él** returned **a** Salt Lake City, careless what became **de su propia vida**, as long as **él** obtained what **él** knew to be justice. There **él** found evil tidings awaiting him. There had been a schism among the Chosen People **unos pocos** months **antes**, some **de los** younger members **de la** Church having rebelled against the authority **de los** Elders, **y** the result had been the secession **de un** certain number **de** the malcontents, who had left Utah **y** become Gentiles. Among these had been Drebber **y** Stangerson; **y nadie** knew whither **ellos** had gone. Rumour reported that Drebber had managed to convert a large part **de su** property into money, **y** that **él** had departed a wealthy man, **mientras su compañero**, Stangerson, was comparatively poor. **No había** clue **para nada, sin embargo**, as to **sus** whereabouts.

Many a man, **sin embargo** vindictive, would have abandoned **todo** thought **de** revenge **en** the face **de tal** a difficulty, **pero** Jefferson Hope never faltered for a moment. **Con la** small competence **él** possessed, eked **fuera por tal** employment as **él** could pick up, **él** travelled **de** town **a** town **a través de** the United States **en** quest **de sus** enemies. Year passed into year, **su** black hair turned grizzled, **pero todavía él** wandered on, a human bloodhound, **con su** mind wholly set upon the one object upon which **él** had devoted **su vida**. At last **su** perseverance **era** rewarded. **Era pero** a glance **de** a face **en** a window, **pero** that one glance told him that Cleveland **en** Ohio possessed **los hombres** whom **él era en** pursuit of. **Él** returned **a su** miserable lodgings **con su** plan **de** vengeance **todo** arranged. **Eso** chanced, **sin embargo**, that

Drebber, looking **desde su** window, had recognized the vagrant **en** the street, **y** had read **asesinato en sus ojos**. **Él** hurried **antes de** a justice **de** the peace, accompanied **por** Stangerson, who had become **su** private secretary, **y** represented **a** him that **ellos estaban en** danger **de sus** lives **de** the jealousy **y** hatred **de un** old rival. That evening Jefferson Hope **fue** taken into custody, **y** not being able to **encontrar** sureties, was detained for some weeks. When at last **él fue** liberated, **era solamente** to **encontrar** that Drebber's house **era** deserted, **y** that **él y su** secretary had departed for Europe.

Again the avenger had been foiled, **y** again **su** concentrated hatred urged him to continue the pursuit. Funds were wanting, **sin embargo**, **y** for some time **él tenía** to return **trabajar**, saving every dollar for **su** approaching journey. At last, having collected enough to keep **vida en** him, **él** departed for Europe, **y** tracked **sus** enemies **de** city **a** city, working **su** way **en cualquier** menial capacity, **pero** never overtaking the fugitives. When **él** reached St. Petersburg **ellos** had departed for Paris; **y** when **él** followed **a ellos** there **él** learned that **ellos había justoo** set off for Copenhagen. At the Danish capital **él era** again **unos pocos días** late, for **ellos** had journeyed on **para** London, **dónde él** at last succeeded **en** running **les** to earth. As to what occurred there, **no podemos hacer** better **que** quote the old hunter's **propio** account, as duly recorded **en** Dr. Watson's Journal, to which **nosotros estamos** already under **tales** obligations.

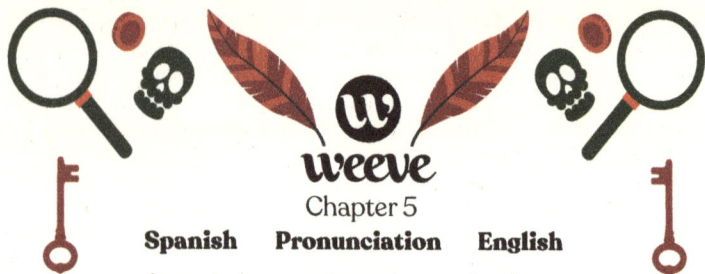

Spanish	Pronunciation	English
solamente	solamente	only
dónde	donde	where
les	les	them
acabarse	akabarse	run out
dos	dos	two
correcta	korekta	right
propio	propjo	own
única cosa	unika kosa	only one thing
donde	donde	where
otros	otros	other
tienen	tjenen	have
justoo	xustoo	just
tales	tales	such

6

A CONTINUATION OF THE REMINISCENCES OF JOHN WATSON, M.D.

Paul Nation, internationally recognized scholar in linguistics, proposes that we pick up most words after reading them in context 12 to 15 times. Sometimes we need only read a word 2 times, but sometimes it takes 30 times- it just depends.

Our prisoner's furious resistance did not apparently indicate **alguna** ferocity **en su** disposition towards ourselves, for **en** finding himself powerless, **él** smiled **en** an affable manner, **y** expressed **sus** hopes that **él** had not hurt <u>**ninguno**</u> **de nosotros en** the scuffle. "**Yo** guess **tú** are going to **llevar** me **a** the police - station," **él** remarked **a** Sherlock Holmes. "My cab's at the door. **Si tú** will loose my legs **yo voy a** walk down **a** it. **Yo** am not **tan** light to lift as **yo** used to be."

Gregson **y** Lestrade exchanged glances as **si ellos** thought this proposition rather a bold one; **pero** Holmes at once took the prisoner at **su** word, **y** loosened the towel which **nosotros** had bound round **sus** ancles. [23] **Él** rose **y** stretched **sus** legs, as though to assure himself that **ellos eran** free once **más**. **Yo** remember that **yo** thought **para** myself, as **yo** eyed him, that **yo había** seldom seen a **más** powerfully built man; **y su** dark sunburned face bore an expression **de** determination **y** energy which **era** as formidable as **su** personal strength.

"**Si** there is a vacant place for a chief **de** the police, **yo** reckon **tú eres** the man for **eso**," **él** said, gazing **con** undisguised admiration at my **compañero** - lodger. "**El camino tú** kept on my trail **era** a caution."

"You had better come **conmigo**," said Holmes **a los dos** detectives.

"**Yo puedo** drive you," said Lestrade.

"**Bien!** y Gregson **puede** come inside **conmigo**. **Tú también**, Doctor, **tú** have taken an interest **en** the case **y** may **también** stick **a nosotros**."

Yo assented gladly, **y nosotros todos** descended together. Our prisoner made no attempt at escape, **pero** stepped calmly into the cab which had been <u>**suyo**</u>, **y nosotros** followed him. Lestrade mounted the box, whipped up the horse, **y** brought **a nosotros en** a **muy** short **tiempo a** our destination. **Nosotros éramos** ushered into a small chamber **donde** a police Inspector noted down our prisoner's name **y** the names **de los hombres con** whose **asesinato él había** been charged. The official **era** a white - faced unemotional man, <u>**quien**</u> went **a través de sus** duties **en** a dull mechanical <u>**manera**</u>. "The prisoner will be put **antes de** the magistrates **en** the course **de** the week," **él** said; "**mientras tanto, señor** Jefferson Hope, have **tú** anything that **tú** wish to say? **Yo debo** warn **te** that **tus palabras** will be taken down, **y** may be used against you."

"**Yo** have got a **buen** deal to say," our prisoner said slowly. "**Yo** want to tell **vosotros** gentlemen **todo sobre eso**."

"Hadn't **tú** better reserve that for **tu** trial?" asked the Inspector.

"**Yo puedo** never be tried," **él** answered. "**Tú** needn't look startled. **Eso** isn't suicide **yo** am thinking of. Are **tú** a Doctor?" **Él** turned **sus** fierce dark **ojos** upon me as **él** asked this last question.

"Yes; **yo** am," **yo** answered.

"**Entonces** put **tu** hand here," **él** said, **con** a smile, motioning **con sus** manacled wrists towards **su** chest.

Yo did **así**; **y** became at once conscious **de un** extraordinary throbbing **y** commotion which was going on inside. The walls **de su** chest seemed to thrill **y** quiver as a frail building <u>**haría**</u> inside **cuando** some powerful engine **era** at **trabajo. En** the silence **de** the room **yo** could hear a dull humming **y** buzzing noise which proceeded **desde el mismo** source.

"**Por qué**," **yo** cried, "**tú tienes** an aortic aneurism!"

"**Eso tiene lo que ellos** call it," **él** said, placidly. "**Yo** went **a un** Doctor last week **sobre eso, y él** told me that **eso** is bound to burst **antes de que muchos días** passed. It has been getting worse for years. **Yo** got **eso de sobre** - exposure **y** under - feeding among the Salt Lake **Montañas. Yo** have done my **trabajo** now, **y yo** don't care **cómo** soon I go, **pero me debería gustar** to leave some account **de** the business behind me. **Yo** don't want to be remembered as a common cut - throat."

The Inspector **y** the **dos** detectives **tenían** a hurried discussion as to the advisability **de** allowing him to tell **su** story.

"Do **tú** consider, Doctor, that there is immediate danger?" the former asked, [24]

"Most certainly there is," **yo** answered.

"**En** that case **eso** is clearly our duty, **en** the interests **de** justice, to **llevar su** statement," said the Inspector. "**Tú estás** at liberty, sir, to give **tu** account, which **yo** again warn **va a** be taken down."

"**Voy a** sit down, **con tu** leave," the prisoner said, suiting the action **a** the word. "This aneurism **de** mine makes me easily tired, **y** the tussle **nosotros tuvimos** half an hour ago has not mended matters. **Yo** am **en** the brink **de** the grave, **y yo** am not likely to lie **a vosotros**. Every word **yo** say is the absolute truth, **y cómo vosotros** use **eso** is a matter **de** no consequence **para** me."

Con estas palabras, Jefferson Hope leaned back **en su** chair **y** began the following remarkable statement. **Él** spoke **en** a calm **y** methodical manner, as though the events which **él** narrated **fueron** commonplace enough. **Yo puedo** vouch for the accuracy **del** subjoined account, for **yo he tenido** access **a** Lestrade's note - book, **en** which the prisoner's **palabras fueron** taken down exactly as **ellas eran** uttered.

"**No es mucho** matter **para vosotros** porqué **yo** hated **estos hombres**," **él** said; "it has enough that **ellos eran** guilty **de** the death **de dos** human beings -- a father **y** a daughter -- **y** that **ellos habían**, therefore, forfeited **su** propias lives. **Después de** the lapse **de tiempo que** has passed since **sus crímenes, era** impossible for me to secure a conviction against **ellos en alguna** court. **Yo** knew **de su** guilt though, **y yo** determined that **yo debería** be judge, jury, **y** executioner **todo** rolled into **uno. Vosotros** habrían have done the **mismo, si vosotros hubierais** any manhood **en vosotros, si vosotros** had been **en** my place.

"That girl that **yo** spoke of was to have married me twenty years ago. She **fue** forced into marrying that **mismo** Drebber, **y** broke **su** heart over it. **Yo** took the marriage ring **de su** dead finger, **y yo** vowed that **sus** dying **ojos deberían** rest upon that very ring, **y** that **sus** last thoughts **deberían** be **del crimen** for which **él era** punished. **Yo** have carried **eso** about **conmigo, y** have followed him **y su** accomplice **sobre dos** continents until **yo** caught **a ellos. Ellos** thought to tire me out, **pero ellos** could **no hacer eso. Si yo** die tomorrow, as is likely enough, **yo** die knowing that my **trabajo en** this **mundo** is done, **y bien** done. **Ellos** have perished, **y por** my hand. There is nothing left for me to hope for, **o** to desire.

"**Ellos eran** rich **y yo era** poor, so that **era** no easy matter for me to follow **les. Cuando yo** got **a** London my **bolsillo era** about empty, **y yo** found that **yo debo** turn my hand **a** something for my living. Driving **y** riding **son** as natural **para** me as walking, **así que yo** applied at a cabowner's office, **y** soon got employment. I was to bring a certain sum a week **a** the owner, **y** whatever **era sobre** that **yo podría** keep for myself. **Había** seldom **mucho** over, **pero yo** managed to scrape along somehow. The hardest job **era** to learn my **camino** about, for **yo** reckon that **de todo** the mazes that ever **fueron** contrived, this city is the **más** confusing. **Tuve** a map beside me though, **y cuando** once **yo** had spotted the principal hotels **y** stations, **yo** got on pretty **bien**.

"**Era a veces antes de que yo** found out **donde** my **dos** gentlemen were living; **pero yo** inquired **y** inquired until at last **yo** dropped across **ellos. Ellos eran** at a boarding - house at Camberwell, over **en el otro** side **de** the river. **Cuando** once **yo** found **a ellos** out **yo** knew that **tuve a ellos** at my mercy. **Yo** had grown my beard, **y no había** chance **de ellos** recognizing me. I would dog **les y** follow **les** until **yo** saw my opportunity. **Era** determined that **ellos deberían** not escape me again.

"**Ellos eran muy** near doing **eso** for **todo** that. **Ir donde ellos harían** about London, **yo era** always at **sus** heels. Sometimes **yo** followed **ellos en** my cab, **y** sometimes **a pie, pero** the former **era** the **mejor,** for **entonces ellos** could not get away **de** me. **Era solamente** early **en** the morning **o** late at night that **yo** could earn anything, so that **yo** began to get behind hand **con** my employer. **Yo** did not mind that, **sin embargo,** as long as **yo** could lay my hand upon **los hombres yo** wanted.

"**Ellos eran muy** cunning, though. **Ellos <u>debían</u>** have thought that **había** some chance **de** their <u>siendo</u> followed, for **ellos** would never **ir fuera** alone, **y** never **después de** nightfall. During **dos** weeks **yo** drove behind **ellos** every day, **y** never once saw **a ellos** separate. Drebber himself **era** drunk half **el tiempo, pero** Stangerson **no estaba** to be caught napping. **Yo** watched **a ellos** late **y** early, **pero** never saw the ghost **de** a chance; **pero yo estaba** not discouraged, for something told me that the hour had almost come. My **<u>único</u>** fear **era** that this thing **en** my chest **podría** burst a little **también** soon **y** leave my **trabajo** undone.

"At last, **una** evening **yo** was driving up **y** down Torquay Terrace, as the street **era** called **en** which **ellos** boarded, **cuando yo** saw a cab drive up **hacia su** door. Presently some luggage **fue** brought **fuera, y después de un momento** Drebber **y** Stangerson followed it, **y** drove off. **Yo** whipped up my horse **y** kept within **vista de ellos,** feeling **muy** ill at ease, for **yo** feared that **ellos** were going to shift **sus** quarters. At Euston Station **ellos** got **fuera, y yo** left a boy to hold my horse, **y** followed **a ellos** on **a** the platform. **Yo** heard **a ellos** ask for the Liverpool train, **y** the guard answer that **uno** had **justo** gone **y** there would not be **otro** for some hours. Stangerson seemed to be put out at that, **pero** Drebber **era** rather pleased **que** otherwise. **Yo** got **tan** close **a ellos en** the bustle that **yo** could hear every word **que** passed **entre ellos**. Drebber said that **él tuvo** a little business **de su** own to **hacer, y** that **si** the **otro esperaría** for him **él** would soon rejoin him. **Su compañero** remonstrated **con él, y** reminded him that **ellos** had resolved to stick together. Drebber answered that the matter **era** a delicate one, **y** that **él debía ir** alone. **Yo** could not catch **qué** Stangerson said **a eso, pero** the **otro** burst out swearing, **y** reminded him that **él era** nothing **más que su** paid servant, **y** that **él debía** not presume to dictate **a** him. **En eso** the Secretary gave it up as a bad job, **y** simply bargained **con él** that **si él** missed the last train **él debería** rejoin him at Halliday's Private Hotel; to which Drebber answered that **él estaría de vuelta en** the platform **antes de** eleven, **y** made **su camino fuera de** the station.

"The moment for which **yo** had waited **tan** long had at last come. **Yo tuve** my enemies within my power. Together **ellos** could protect **cada otro, pero** singly **ellos estaban** at my mercy. **Yo** did not act, **sin embargo, con** undue precipitation. My plans **estaban** already formed. There is no satisfaction **en** vengeance unless the offender **tiene tiempo** to realize **quien** it is that strikes him, **y por qué** retribution has come upon him. **Tuve** my plans arranged by which **yo debería tener** the opportunity **de** making the man **quien** had wronged me understand that **su** old sin had found him out. **Eso** chanced that **algunos días antes de que un caballero quien** had been engaged **en** looking over some houses **en** the Brixton Road had dropped the key **de uno de ellos en** my carriage. **Era** claimed that **misma** evening, **y** returned; **pero en** the interval **yo** had taken a moulding **de eso, y tenía** a duplicate constructed. By means **de** this **yo tuve** access **a** at least **un** spot **en** this **gran** city **dónde yo** could rely upon **siendo** free **de** interruption. **Cómo** to get Drebber **a** that house **era** the difficult problem which **yo tuve** now to solve.

"**Él** walked down the road **y** went into **uno o dos** liquor shops, staying for nearly half - an - hour **en** the last **de ellos. Cuando él** came **fuera él** staggered in **su** walk, **y fue** evidently pretty **bien** on. **Hubo** a hansom **justo en** front **de mí, y él** hailed **eso. Yo** followed **eso tan** close that the nose **de** my horse **era** within a yard **de su** driver the whole **camino. Nosotros** rattled across Waterloo Bridge **y mediante** miles **de** streets, until, **para** my astonishment, **nosotros** found ourselves back **en** the Terrace **en** which **él** had boarded. **Yo** could not imagine **qué su** intention **era** in returning there; **pero yo** went on **y** pulled up my cab a hundred yards **o así de** the house. **Él** entered it, **y su** hansom drove away. Give me a glass **de agua, si** you please. My mouth gets dry **con** the talking."

Yo handed him the glass, **y él** drank **eso** down.

"**Eso** is better," **él** said. "**Bien, yo** waited for a quarter **de** an hour, **o más, cuando** suddenly there came a noise **como gente** struggling inside the house. Next moment the door **fue** flung open **y dos hombres** appeared, **uno de** whom **era** Drebber, **y** the **otro era** a young chap whom I had never seen **antes**. This **compañero tenía** Drebber **por** the collar, **y cuando ellos** came **a** the head **de los pasos él** gave him a shove **y** a kick which sent him half across the road. '**Tú** hound,' **él** cried, shaking **su** stick at him; '**voy a** teach **a ti** to insult an honest girl!' **Él era tan** hot that **creo él <u>habría</u>** thrashed Drebber **con su** cudgel, **solamente** that the cur staggered away down the road as fast as **sus** legs **le llevarían. Él** ran as far as the corner, **y entonces**, seeing my cab, **él** hailed me **y** jumped in. 'Driveme **a** Halliday's Private Hotel,' said **él**.

"**Cuando yo tuve** him fairly inside my cab, my heart jumped **tan con** joy that **yo** feared lest at this last moment my aneurism **podria ir** wrong. **Yo** drove along slowly, weighing **en** my **propia** mind **qué era mejor** to **hacer. Podría tomar** him right out into the country, **y** there **en** some deserted lane **tener** my last interview **con él. Yo tuve** almost decided upon this, **cuando él** solved the problem for me. The craze for drink had seized him again, **y él** ordered me to pull up outside a gin palace. **Él** went in, leaving word that **yo debería** wait for him. There **él** remained until closing **tiempo, y cuando él** came **fuera él era tan** far gone that **yo** knew the game **era en** my **propias manos**.

"Don't imagine that **yo** intended to kill him **en** cold blood. <u>**Sería solamente**</u> have been rigid justice **si yo** had done **así, pero yo** could not bring myself to **hacer eso. Yo tuve** long determined that **debería tener** a show for **su vida si él** chose to **llevar** advantage **de eso**. Among the **muchos** billets which **yo** have filled in America during my wandering **vida, era** once janitor **y** sweeper out **de** the laboratory at York College. **Un** day the professor was lecturing **sobre** poisions, [25] **y él** showed **sus** students some alkaloid, as **él** called **eso**, which **él** had extracted **de algunos** South American arrow poison, **y** which **era tan** powerful that the least grain meant <u>**muerte instantánea. Yo**</u> spotted the bottle **en** which this preparation **era** kept, **y cuando ellos eran todos** gone, **yo** helped myself **a un** little **de** it. **Yo era** a fairly **buen** dispenser, **así que yo** worked this alkaloid into small, soluble pills, **y cada** pill **yo** put **en** a box **con un** similar pill made without the poison. **Yo** determined at **el tiempo** that **cuando yo tuve** my chance, my gentlemen **deberían** each **tener** a draw **fuera de uno de** these boxes, **mientras yo** ate the pill **que** remained. **Sería** quite as deadly, **y** a **buen** deal less noisy **que** firing across a handkerchief. **Desde** that day **yo tuve** always my pill boxes about **conmigo, y el tiempo** had now come **cuando** I was to use **los**.

"It was nearer **una que** twelve, **y** a wild, bleak night, blowing hard **y** raining **en** torrents. Dismal as **era** outside, **yo era** glad within -- **tan** glad that **yo** could have shouted out **de** pure exultation. **Si cualquiera de vosotros** gentlemen have ever pined for a thing, **y** longed for **eso** during twenty long years, **y entonces** suddenly found **eso** within **tu** reach, **vosotros entenderíais** my feelings. **Yo** lit a cigar, **y** puffed at **eso** to steady my nerves, **pero** my **manos** were trembling, **y** my temples throbbing **con** excitement. As **yo** drove, **yo** could **ver** old John Ferrier **y** sweet Lucy looking at me **fuera de** the darkness **y** smiling at me, **justo como** plain as **yo veo a vosotros todos en** this room. **Todo el camino ellos estaban** ahead **de mí, uno en cada** side **de** the horse until **yo** pulled up at the house **en** the Brixton Road.

"**No había** a soul to be seen, nor a sound to be heard, except the dripping **de** the rain. **Cuando yo** looked in at the window, **yo** found Drebber **todo** huddled together **en** a drunken sleep. **Yo** shook him **por** the arm, 'It is <u>**hora**</u> to get **fuera**,' **yo** said.

"'**Muy bien**, cabby,' said **él**.

"**Yo** suppose **él** thought **nosotros** had come **a** the hotel that **él** had mentioned, for **él** got **fuera** without **otra** word, **y** followed me down the garden. **Yo tenía** to walk beside him to keep him steady, for **él era todavía** a little top - heavy. **Cuando nosotros** came **a** the door, **yo** opened **eso, y** led him into the front room. **Yo** give **a vosotros** my word that **todo el camino**, the father **y** the daughter were walking **en** front **de nosotros**.

"'**Eso** is infernally dark,' said **él**, stamping about.

"'Wewill soon **tener** a light,' **yo** said, striking a match **y** putting **eso hacia** a wax candle which **yo** had brought **conmigo**. 'Now, Enoch Drebber,' **yo** continued, turning **a** him, **y** holding the light **a** my **propia** face, '<u>**quién**</u> am **yo**?'

"**Él** gazed at me **con** bleared, drunken **ojos** for a moment, **y entonces yo** saw a horror spring up **en ellos, y** convulse **sus** whole features, which showed me that **él** knew me. **Él** staggered back **con una** livid face, **y yo** saw the perspiration break out upon **su** brow, **mientras sus** teeth chattered **en su** head. At **la vista, yo** leaned my back against the door **y** laughed loud **y** long. **Tuve** always known that vengeance **sería** sweet, **pero tuve** never hoped for the contentment **de** soul which now possessed me.

"'**Tú** dog!' **Yo** said; '**yo** have hunted **a ti desde** Salt Lake City **hasta** St. Petersburg, **y tú has** always escaped me. Now, at last **tus** wanderings have come **a** an end, for either you **o yo** shall never **ver** tomorrow's sun rise.' **Él** shrunk still further away as **yo** spoke, **y yo** could **ver en su** face that **él** thought **yo estaba** mad. **Así lo estaba por el momento** . The pulses **en** my temples beat **como** sledge - hammers, **y yo** believe **yo habría tenido** a fit **de**

algún sort **si** the blood had not gushed **de** my nose **y** relieved me.

"'**Qué piensas de** Lucy Ferrier now?' **Yo** cried, locking the door, **y** shaking the key **en su** face. 'Punishmenthas been slow **en** coming, **pero eso** has overtaken **a ti** at last.' **Yo** saw **sus** coward **labios** tremble as **yo** spoke. **Él habría** begged for **su vida, pero él** knew **bien** that **era** useless.

"**Me matarías ?** " **Él** stammered.

"'Thereis no **asesinato,' yo** answered. '**Quién** talks **de** murdering a mad dog? **Qué** mercy **tenías tú** upon my poor darling, **cuando tú** dragged **a ella de su** slaughtered father, **y** bore **a ella** away **a tu** accursed **y** shameless harem.'

"'**No era yo quien** killed **su** father,' **él** cried.

"'**Pero** it was **tú quien** broke **su** innocent heart,' **yo** shrieked, thrusting the box **antes de** him. 'Letthe high God judge **entre nosotros.** Choose **y** eat. There is death **en uno y vida en** the **otro. Yo** shall **llevar** what **tú** leave. Let **nosotros ver si** there is justice upon the earth, **o si nosotros estamos** ruled **por** chance.'

"**Él** cowered away **con** wild cries **y** prayers for mercy, **pero yo** drew my knife **y** held it **hacia su** throat until **él** had obeyed me. **Entonces yo** swallowed the **otro, y nosotros** stood facing **uno al otro en** silence for a minute **o más**, waiting to **ver** which **iba** to live **y** which **iba** to die. Shall **yo** ever forget **la mirada** which came **sobre su** face **cuando** the **primer** warning pangs told him that the poison **era en su** system? **Yo** laughed as **yo** saw **eso, y** held Lucy's marriage ring **en** front **de sus ojos.** It was but for a moment, for the action **de** the alkaloid is rapid. A spasm **de** pain contorted **sus** features; **él** threw **sus manos fuera en** front **de él**, staggered, **y entonces, con un** hoarse cry, fell heavily upon the floor. **Yo** turned him over **con** my foot, **y** placed my hand upon **su** heart. **No había** movement. **Él estaba** dead!

"The blood had been streaming **de** my nose, **pero yo** had taken no notice **de eso. No sé qué era** that put it into my head to write upon the wall **con eso.** Perhaps **fue** some mischievous idea **de** setting the police upon a wrong track, for **yo** felt light - hearted **y** cheerful. **Yo** remembered a German **siendo** found **en** New York **con** Rache written up above him, **y era** argued at **el tiempo en** the newspapers that the secret societies **debe** have done **eso. Yo** guessed that what puzzled the New Yorkers would puzzle the Londoners, **así que yo** dipped my finger **en** my **propia** blood **y** printed **eso en un** convenient place **en** the wall. **Entonces yo** walked down **hacia** my cab **y** found that **no había nadie** about, **y** that the night **era todavía muy** wild. **Yo** had driven some distance **cuando yo** put my hand into **el bolsillo en** which **yo** usually kept Lucy's ring, **y** found that **no estaba** there. I was thunderstruck at this, for **era** the **único** memento that **tuve de ella.** Thinking that

yo podría have dropped **eso cuando yo** stooped **sobre** Drebber's body, **yo** drove back, **y** leaving my cab **en** a side street, **yo** went boldly up **hacia** the house -- for **yo estaba** ready to dare anything rather **que** lose the ring. **Cuando yo** arrived there, **yo** walked right into the arms **de** a police - officer **quien** was coming **fuera, y solamente** managed to disarm **sus** suspicions by pretending to be hopelessly drunk.

"**Eso fue cómo** Enoch Drebber came **a su** end. **Todo** I had to **hacer entonces era** to **hacer** as much for Stangerson, **y así** pay off John Ferrier's debt. **Yo** knew that **él** was staying at Halliday's Private Hotel, **y yo** hung about **todo** day, **pero él** never came **fuera.** [26] fancy that **él** suspected something **cuando** Drebber failed to put in an appearance. **Él estaba** cunning, was Stangerson, **y** always **en su** guard. **Si él** thought **él** could keep me off by staying indoors **él estaba muy** much mistaken. **Yo** soon found out which **era** the window **de su** bedroom, **y** early next morning **yo** took advantage **de algunas** ladders which were lying **en** the lane behind the hotel, **y así** made my **camino** into **su** room **en** the grey **de** the dawn. **Yo** woke him up **y** told him that the hour had come **cuando él** was to answer for **la vida él** had taken **tan** long **antes. Yo** described Drebber's death **a** him, **y yo** gave him the **misma** choice **de las** poisoned pills. Instead **de** grasping at the chance **de** safety which **eso** offered him, **él** sprang **de su** bed **y** flew at my throat. **En** self - defence **yo** stabbed him **a** the heart. **Eso habría sido** the **mismo en algún** case, for Providence would never have allowed **su** guilty hand to pick out anything but the poison.

"**Yo tengo** little **más** to say, **y eso** is as **bien,** for **yo** am about done up. **Yo** went on cabbing **eso** for a day **o así,** intending to keep at **eso** until **yo** could save enough to **llevar** me back **a** America. **Yo** was standing **en** the yard **cuando** a ragged youngster asked **si había** a cabby there called Jefferson Hope, **y** said that **su** cab **era** wanted **por un caballero** at 221B, Baker Street. **Yo** went round, suspecting no harm, **y** the next thing **yo** knew, this young man here **tenía** the bracelets **en** my wrists, **y** as neatly snackled [27] as ever **yo** saw **en** my **vida. Eso** is the whole **de** my story, gentlemen. **Podeis** consider me to be a murderer; **pero yo** hold that **yo** am **justo como mucho** an officer **de** justice as **vosotros sois.**"

Tan thrilling had the man's narrative been, **y su** manner **era tan** impressive that **nosotros** had sat silent **y** absorbed. **Incluso** the professional detectives, blasé as **ellos eran en** every detail **del crimen,** appeared to be keenly interested **en** the man's story. **Cuando él** finished **nosotros** sat for some minutes **en** a stillness which **era solamente** broken **por** the scratching **de** Lestrade's pencil as **él** gave the finishing touches **a su** shorthand account.

"There is **sólo un** point **en** which **me debería gustar** a little

más information," Sherlock Holmes said at last. "**Quién era tu** accomplice who came for the ring which **yo** advertised?"

The prisoner winked at my friend jocosely. "**Yo puedo** tell my **propios** secrets," **él** said, "**pero yo** don't get **otra gente** into trouble. **Yo** saw **tu** advertisement, **y yo** thought **podría ser** a plant, **o podría ser** the ring which **yo** wanted. My friend volunteered to **ir y ver. Creo que reconocerás que lo hizo inteligentemente** . "

"**No** a doubt **de eso**," said Holmes heartily.

"Now, gentlemen," the Inspector remarked gravely, "the forms **de** the law **deben** be complied with. **En** Thursday the prisoner will be brought **antes de** the magistrates, **y tu** attendance **será** required. Until **entonces yo seré** responsible for him." **Él** rang the bell as **él** spoke, **y** Jefferson Hope was led off **por** a couple **de** warders, **mientras** my friend **y yo** made **nuestra camino fuera de la** Station **y** took a cab back **a** Baker Street.

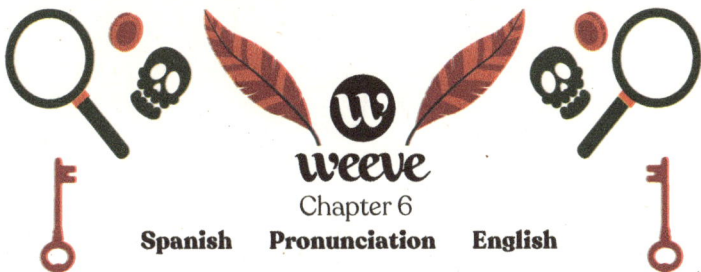

Chapter 6

Spanish	Pronunciation	English
ninguno	ningwno	any
suyo	suio	his
quien	kjen	who
manera	manera	way
te	te	you
haría	arja	would do
porqué	porke	why
propias	propjas	own
habrían	abrjan	would
debían	debjan	must
siendo	sjendo	being
único	uniko	only
esperaría	esperarja	would wait
misma	misma	same
mediante	medjante	through
habría	abrja	would have
sería	serja	it would
muerte instantánea	mwerte instantanea	instant death
hora	ora	time

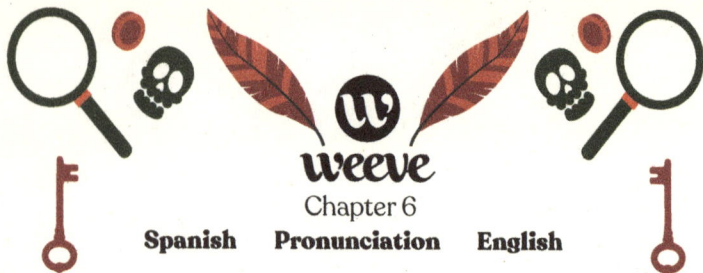

Spanish	Pronunciation	English
quién	kjen	who
tenías	tenjas	had
debe	debe	must
propios	propjos	own
será	sera	will be

7

THE CONCLUSION

"Vocabulary is no different than any other system or part of language, we acquired it the same way, by understanding messages, by reading them or by listening to them." – Jeff McQuillan, senior researcher at Center for Educational Development, Inc.

Tuvimos todos been warned to appear **antes de** the magistrates upon the Thursday; **pero cuando** the Thursday came **no hubo** occasion **para** our testimony. A higher Judge had taken the matter **en** hand, **y** Jefferson Hope had been summoned **antes** a tribunal **donde** strict justice **sería** meted out **a** him. **En la** very night **después su** capture the aneurism burst, **y él fue** found **en** the morning stretched upon the floor **de** the cell, **con un** placid smile upon **su** face, **como** though **él había sido** able **en su** dying moments to **mirar** back upon a useful **vida, y en trabajo bien** done.

"Gregson **y** Lestrade **estarán** wild **sobre su** death," Holmes remarked, **como nosotros** chatted **eso** over next evening. "**Dónde** will **su** grand advertisement be now?"

"No veo que hayan tenido mucho que ver con su captura" , **respondí** .

"Qué tú haces en este mundo es a matter **de** no consequence," returned **mi acompañante**, bitterly. "The question **es, qué** can you make **gente** believe that **vosotros** have done. Never mind," **él** continued, **más** brightly, **después de** a pause. "**Yo no habría** missed the investigation **por** anything. **No ha habido** better case within **mi** recollection. Simple **como era, habían** several most instructive points **sobre eso.**"

"Simple!" **Yo** ejaculated.

"**Bueno**, really, **puede** hardly be described **como** otherwise," said Sherlock Holmes, smiling **a mi** surprise. "The proof **de su** intrinsic simplicity **es**, that without **ninguna ayuda** save **unos pocos muy** ordinary deductions I was able to lay **mi** hand upon the criminal within three **días**."

"**Eso es** true," said **yo**.

"**Yo tengo** already explained **a ti** that **qué es fuera de lo** common **es** usually a guide rather **que** a hindrance. **En** solving a problem **de** this sort, the grand thing **es** to be able to reason backwards. **Eso es** a **muy** useful accomplishment, **y** a **muy** easy one, **pero gente** do not practise **eso mucho**. **En** the every - day affairs **de vida es más** useful to reason forwards, **y así** the **otro** comes to be neglected. **Hay** fifty who **pueden** reason synthetically **por uno** who **puede** reason analytically."

"**Yo** confess," said **yo**, "that **yo no** quite follow **a ti**."

"**Yo** hardly expected that **lo harías**. Let me **ver si yo puedo** make **eso** clearer. **La mayoría de la gente**, **si tú** describe a train **de** events **a ellos**, **te dirán** what the result **sería**. **Ellos pueden** put **aquellos** events together **en sus** minds, **y** argue **de ellos** that something will come to pass. **Hay pocas personas, sin embargo, quienes**, **si tú** told **a ellos** a result, **serían capaces** to evolve **de sus propias** inner consciousness what **los pasos fueron** which led up **a** that result. This power **es lo que yo** mean **cuando yo** talk **de** reasoning backwards, **o** analytically."

"**Yo** understand," said **yo**.

"Now **esto era** a case **en el cual** you were given the result **y** had to **encontrar** everything else **por** yourself. Now let me endeavour to show **te** the different **pasos en mi** reasoning. To begin at the beginning. **Yo** approached the house, **como tú sabes, a pie, y con mi** mind entirely free **de toda** impressions. **Yo** naturally began **por** examining the roadway, **y allí, como yo he** already explained **a ti**, **yo** saw clearly the marks **de** a cab, **las cuales**, **yo** ascertained **por** inquiry, **debe haber sido allí** during the night. **Yo** satisfied myself that **era** a cab **y no** a private carriage **por el** narrow gauge **de** the wheels. The ordinary London growler **es** considerably less wide **que un** gentleman's brougham.

"**Esto era** the **primer** point gained. **Yo entonces** walked slowly down the garden path, **el cual** happened to be composed **de** a clay soil, peculiarly suitable **para** taking impressions. **Ninguna duda eso** appeared **para ti** to **ser** a mere trampled line **de** slush, **pero para mis** trained **ojos** every mark upon **su** surface **tenía** a meaning. **No hay** branch **de detective** science **la cual es tan** important **y tan** much neglected **como** the art **de** tracing footsteps. Happily, **yo he** always laid **gran** stress upon **eso, y mucha** practice has made **eso** second nature **para** me. **Yo** saw the heavy footmarks **de** the constables, **pero yo** saw also the track **de los dos hombres quienes** had **primero** passed **a través de** the garden. **Era** easy to tell that **ellos habian estado antes de** the others, **porque en** places **sus** marks had been entirely obliterated **por** the others coming upon the top **de ellos. En esta manera mi** second link **era** formed, **la cual** told me that the nocturnal visitors **fueron dos en** number, **uno** remarkable **por su** height (**como yo** calculated **de** the length **de su** stride), **y** the **otro** fashionably dressed, to judge **de la** small **y** elegant impression left **por su** boots.

"On entering the house this last inference **fue** confirmed. **Mi bien** - booted man lay **antes de** me. The tall one, **entonces**, had done **el asesinato, si asesinato** there was. **No había** wound upon the dead man's person, **pero** the agitated expression upon **su** face assured me that **él** had foreseen su fate **antes de eso** came upon him. **Hombres quienes** die **de** heart disease, **o cualquier** sudden natural **porque**, never **por** any chance exhibit agitation upon **sus** features. Having sniffed the dead man's **labios yo** detected a slightly sour smell, **y yo** came **a** the conclusion that **él había** had poison forced upon him. Again, **yo** argued that **él había** been forced upon him **de** the hatred **y** fear expressed upon **su** face. **Por** the method **de** exclusion, **yo** had arrived **a** this result, **por ninguna otra** hypothesis would meet the facts. Do not imagine that **fue** a **muy** unheard **de** idea. The forcible administration **de** poison **es por** no means a **nueva** thing **en** criminal annals. The cases **de** Dolsky **en** Odessa, **y de** Leturier **en** Montpellier, **ocurrirán enseguida a cualquier** toxicologist.

"**Y** now came the **gran** question **como** to the reason **por qué**. Robbery **no había sido** the object **del asesinato, porque** nothing **fue** taken. Was it politics, **entonces, o fue** it a woman? **Esa era** the question **la cual** confronted me. **Yo estaba** inclined **desde la primera a la** latter supposition. Political assassins **están** only **también** glad to **hacer su trabajo y** to fly. **Este asesinato** had, **por el contrario**, been done most deliberately, **y** the perpetrator had left **sus** tracks **por todas partes de** the room, showing that **él había estado allí todo el tiempo. Debe haber sido** a private wrong, **y no** a political one, **lo cual** called **para** such a methodical revenge. **Cuando** the inscription **fue** discovered upon the wall **yo estaba más** inclined **que** ever **a mi** opinion. The thing **era también** evidently a blind. **Cuando** the ring **fue** found, **sin embargo, eso** settled the question. Clearly the murderer had used **eso** to remind **su** victim **de** some dead **o** absent woman. **Fue en este punto** that **yo** asked Gregson whether **él** had enquired **en su** telegram **a** Cleveland **como a cualquier** particular point **en** Mr. Drebber's former career. **Él** answered, **tú** remember, **en** the negative.

"**Yo entonces** proceeded to make a careful examination **de** the room, **la cual** confirmed me **en mi** opinion **como para** the murderer's height, **y** furnished me **con el** additional details **como** to the Trichinopoly cigar **y** the length **de sus** nails. **Yo había** already come **a** the conclusion, since **no habían** signs **de** a struggle, that the blood **la cual** covered the floor had burst **de** the murderer's nose **en su** excitement. **Yo** could perceive that the track **de** blood coincided **con** the track **de sus pies**. **Es** seldom that **ningún** man, unless **él es muy** full - blooded, breaks out **en esta manera a través de** emotion, **así que yo** hazarded the opinion that the criminal **era** probably a robust **y** ruddy - faced man. Events proved that **yo** had judged correctly.

"Having left the house, **yo** proceeded to **hacer** what Gregson had neglected. **Yo** telegraphed **a** the head **de** the police **en** Cleveland, limiting **mi** enquiry **a** the circumstances connected **con** the marriage **de** Enoch Drebber. The answer **fue** conclusive. It told me that Drebber had already applied **para** the protection **de** the law against an old rival **en** love, named Jefferson Hope, **y** that this **mismo** Hope **estaba a** present **en** Europe. **Yo** knew now that **yo** held the clue **hacia el misterio en mi** hand, **y todo eso** remained **era** to secure the murderer.

"**Yo había** already determined **en mi propia** mind that the man **quien** had walked into the house **con** Drebber, was none **otro que** the man **quien** had driven the cab. The marks **en** the road showed me that the horse had wandered on **en un manera la cual habría sido** impossible had there been anyone **en** charge **de eso**. **Dónde, entonces**, could the driver be, unless **él estuviera** inside the house? Again, **es** absurd to suppose that **ningún** sane man **realizaría** a deliberate **crimen** under the very **ojos, como si fuera, de una** third person, **quien** was sure to betray him. Lastly, supposing **un** man wished to dog **otro a través de** London, **qué** better means could **él** adopt **que** to turn cabdriver. **Todas** these considerations led me **a la** irresistible conclusion that Jefferson Hope **iba** to be found among the jarveys **de la** Metropolis.

"**Si él había sido** one **no había** reason to believe that **él** had ceased to be. **Al contrario, de su** point **de** view, **cualquier** sudden change **sería** likely to draw attention **a** himself. **Él** would, probably, **por un momento al menos**, continue to perform **sus** duties. **No había** reason to suppose that **él** was going under an assumed name. **Por qué debería él** change **su** name **en** a country **donde nadie** knew **su** original one? **Yo** therefore organized **mi** Street Arab **detective** corps, **y** sent **a ellos** systematically **haciaa** every cab proprietor **en** London until **ellos** ferreted out the man that **yo** wanted. **Cómo bien ellos** succeeded, **y cómo** quickly **yo** took advantage **de eso**, are **todavía** fresh **en tu** recollection. **El asesinaato de** Stangerson **fue** an incident **el cual fue** entirely unexpected, **pero el cual** could hardly **en cualquier** case have been prevented. **A través de eso, como tú sabes, yo** came into possession **de** the pills, the existence **de las cuales yo había** already surmised. **Verás** the whole thing **es** a chain **de** logical sequences without a break **o** flaw."

"**Es** wonderful!" Yo cried. "**Tus** merits **deberían ser** publicly recognized. **Deberías** publish an account **de** the case. **Si tú no lo haces** , yo lo haré por ti . "

" **Puede hacer lo que quiera , doctor**" , respondió . "Mira here!" Él continued, handing a paper over **para** me, "**mira a esto!**"

Era the Echo **para** the day, **y** the paragraph to **el cual él** pointed **era** devoted **a** the case **en** question.

"The public," **eso** said, "have lost a sensational treat **a través de** the sudden death **de** the man Hope, **quien era** suspected **del asesinato de el señor** Enoch Drebber **y de el señor** Joseph Stangerson. The details **de** the case will probably be never known now, though **nosotros estamos** informed upon good authority that **el crimen fue** the result **de un** old standing **y** romantic feud, **en** which love **y** Mormonism bore a part. It seems that both the victims belonged, **en sus** younger **días, a los** Latter Day Saints, **y** Hope, the deceased prisoner, hails also **de** Salt Lake City. **Si** the case **ha tenido no otro** effect, it, **al menos**, brings out **en la mayor** striking manner the efficiency **de nuestro detective** police force, **y servirá como** a lesson **a todos** foreigners that **ellos harán** wisely to settle **sus** feuds **en** home, **y** not to carry **los** on **a** British soil. **Es** an open secret that the credit **de esta** smart capture belongs entirely **a los bien** - known Scotland Yard officials, Messrs. Lestrade **y** Gregson. The man **fue** apprehended, **eso** appears, **en** the rooms **de un** certain **señor** Sherlock Holmes, **quien** has himself, **como** an amateur, shown some talent **en la detective** line, **y quien, con tales** instructors, may hope **en tiempo** to attain **para algún** degree **de sus** skill. **Es** expected that a testimonial **de algún** sort **será** presented **a los dos** officers **como un** fitting recognition **de sus** services."

"Did not **yo** tell **a ti así cuando nosotros** started?" cried Sherlock Holmes **con** a laugh. "**Eso es** the result **de todo** our Study **en** Scarlet: to get **les** a testimonial!"

"Never mind," **yo** answered, "**yo tengo todos** the facts **en mi** journal, **y** the public shall **saber los. En** the meantime **tú debes** make yourself contented **por** the consciousness **de** success, **como** the Roman miser--

"'Populusme sibilat, at mihi plaudo Ipse domi simul ac nummos contemplor in arca.'"

La Fine

Felicidades on completing your weeve! We hoped you enjoyed the process and you feel like you have a **aprendió mucho**. Remember that **aprendizaje de idiomas** is a long journey. Keep on reading your weeves and you will be a Spanish speaking Sherlock Holmes **en poco tiempo**! If you felt this **libro** helped you **realmente apreciaríamos** a review on Amazon, our website or goodreads. It helps **más personas** like yourself find our weeves. **Muchas gracias** for your support!

- Evan, Cian and Oisin

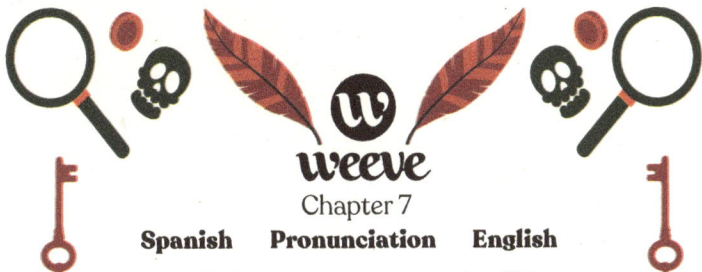

Spanish	Pronunciation	English
estarán	estaran	will be
mi acompañante	mi akompaɲante	my companion
bueno	bweno	well
quienes	kjenes	who
serían capaces	serjan kapases	would be able
allí	aji	there
mis	mis	my
mucha	mut͡ʃa	much
ocurrirán	okuriran	will occur
enseguida	ensegida	at once
realizaría	realisarja	would carry out
haciaa	asiaa	to
verás	beras	you see
servirá	serbira	will serve

GLOSSARY

A

a // a // to
acabarse // akabarse // run out
adios // adjos // good
adiós // adjos // good
agua // agwa // water
al // al // to the
alguien // algien // some one
alguna // algwna // any
allí // aji // there
aquellas // akejas // those
asesinato // asesinato // murder
aunque // aunke // even though
ayuda // aiuda // help
ayudar // aiudar // help

B

buen // bwen // good
bueno // bweno // well
buenos // bwenos // good

C

cada // kada // each
cazador // kasador // hunter
como mucho // komo mutʃo // most
con // kon // with
conmigo // konmigo // with me
contigo // kontigo // with you
correcta // korekta // right
cosas // kosas // things
creo // kreo // i think
cualquiera // kwalkjera // any
cuantas // kwantas // how many
cómo // komo // how

D

date prisa // date prisa // hurry on
de // de // from
debe // debe // must
debería // deberja // should
deberíamos // deberjamos // we should
deberían // deberjan // should
deberías // deberjas // you should

debían // debjan // must
del // del // of the
descubrir // deskubrir // find out
detective // detektibe // detective
donde // donde // where
dos // dos // two
días // djas // days
dónde // donde // where

E

ellas // ejas // them
en // en // in
encontrar // enkontrar // find
enseguida // ensegida // at once
entonces // entonses // then
entre // entre // between
era // era // was
eran // eran // were
esa // esa // that
ese tipo // ese tipo // that fellow
eso // eso // it
esperaría // esperarja // would wait
estaba // estaba // was
estaban // estaban // were
estabas // estabas // you were
estamos // estamos // are
estarán // estaran // will be
estsba // estsba // was
estábamos // estabamos // we were
están // estan // are

F

fuera // fwera // out
fueron // fweron // were
fui // fwi // was
fuimos // fwimos // were

G

gente // xente // people
gracias // grasias // thank you
gran // gran // great
grandes // grandes // great

H

ha sido // a sido // it has been
habría // abrja // would have
habrían // abrjan // would
había // abja // there was

hacemos // asemos // we do
hacen // asen // do
hacer // aser // do
hacia // asia // to
haciaa // asiaa // to
haría // arja // would do
hasta // asta // to
hay // ai // there are
hora // ora // time
hubo // wbo // there was

I

iba // iba // was
incluso // inkluso // even
instante // instante // instant
ir // ir // go

J

justo // xusto // just
justoo // xustoo // just

L

labios // labjos // lips
le // le // her
les // les // them
llevad // jebad // take
llevar // jebar // take
luego // lwego // then

M

manera // manera // way
mayor // maior // most
mayoría // maiorja // most
mediante // medjante // through
mejor // mexor // best
mi acompañante // mi akom-
pañante // my companion
mientras // mjentras // while
mira // mira // look
mirar // mirar // look
mis // mis // my
misma // misma // same
mismo // mismo // same
montañas // montañas // mountains
mucha // mutʃa // much
muchos // mutʃos // many
muerte instantánea // mwerte
instantanea // instant death

mundo // mundo // world
muy bien // mui bjen // all

N

nadie // nadje // no one
ninguna // ningwna // any
ninguno // ningwno // any
ningún // ningwn // any
nosotros // nosotros // we
nuevo // nwebo // new
nuevos // nwebos // new

O

o // o // or
ocurrirán // okuriran // will occur
otra // otra // another
otras // otras // other
otro // otro // another
otros // otros // other

P

palabras // palabras // words
para // para // to
parecer // pareser // look
pasos // pasos // steps
pensar // pensar // think
pero // pero // but
pies // pjes // feet
podemos // podemos // we can
podría // podrja // might
podríamos // podrjamos // might
podrían // podrjan // might
podrías // podrjas // you might
por supuesto // por supwesto // of
course
porque // porke // because
porqué // porke // why
primer // primer // first
primera // primera // first
primero // primero // first
propias // propjas // own
propio // propjo // own
propios // propjos // own
puedía estar // pwedja estar // might
be

Q

que // ke // that

quien // kjen // who
quienes // kjenes // who
quién // kjen // who

R

realizaría // realisarja // would
carry out

S

saber // saber // know
ser // ser // being
servirá // serbira // will serve
será // sera // will be
sería // serja // it would
serían capaces // serjan kapases //
would be able
si // si // if
siendo // sjendo // being
sin embargo // sin embargo //
however
sobre // sobre // about
sois // sois // are
solamente // solamente // only
solo // solo // just
somos // somos // are
son // son // are
su // su // his
suyo // suio // his
sé // se // i know

T

tal // tal // such
tales // tales // such
también // tambjen // too
tan // tan // so
tantas // tantas // so
tanto // tanto // so much
tantos // tantos // so
te // te // you
tenemos // tenemos // have
tener // tener // have
tenía // tenja // had
tenían // tenjan // had
tenías // tenjas // had
tiene // tjene // has
tienen // tjenen // have
todas // todas // all
todavía // todabja // still

todos // todos // all
trabajar // trabaxar // work
trabajo // trabaxo // work
tu encuentras // tu enkwentras // you
find
tuve // tube // i had
tuvimos // tubimos // we had
tú // tu // you

U

unas pocas // unas pokas // a few
unos pocos // unos pokos // a few
usted // usted // you

V

van // ban // go
verás // beras // you see
vete // bete // you go
vista // bista // sight
vosotros // bosotros // you

Y

y // i // and
yo // io // i
you // iou // you

Ú

única cosa // unika kosa // only one
thing
único // uniko // only

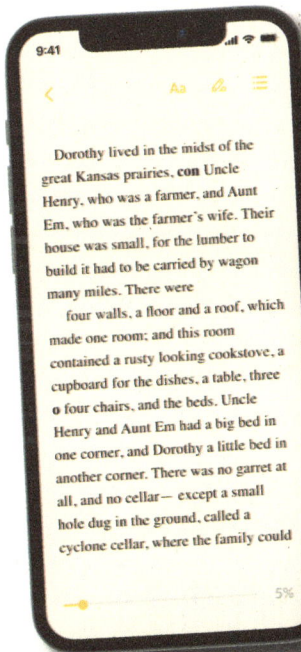

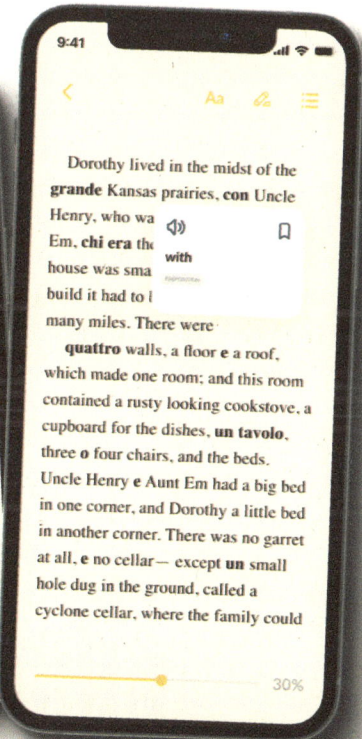